Modern Efik

A concise introduction to the Efik language

kasahorow

Everyone is an African
Revised 2022-08-01
© 2011
KWID: G-KKK25-EFI-EN-2022-08-01

Nana Akua, Kwesi Kwaa Prah

Contents

Preface — 7
    Sharing License 7
    Errata 8

Modern Iko Mbakara — 9
    Before you jump in 10
    Let's go! 11
    All the words you need 11

Read Modern Iko Mbakara — 13

Write Modern Iko Mbakara — 17
    Spelling 17
    Write for comprehension 17
    Importing foreign words 18
    Punctuation 18

Speaking Iko Mbakara — 21

Use These Words — 23
    Simple Pronouns 23
        Ownership 23

Nouns	24
Adjectives	25
Verbs	25
Adverbs	25
Conjunctions	26
Exclamations	26
Basic Ideas	26
Numbers	26
Time	28
Days of the week	28
Months of the year	29
Directions	30
Food	30
Transport	31
Colours	31
Family	31
Occupations	32
Actions	32
Write and speak Iko Mbakara!	34

Basic Iko Mbakara Reading	**45**
Basic Iko Mbakara Phrases	**47**
Greetings	47
Respect	47
Request	48
Answer	48
Basic Iko Mbakara Translation	**51**
[Kw:Efi]-English	**57**
Index	**143**

Preface

kasahorow loves Iko Mbakara

Our mission is to teach inclusion.

The first step to inclusive Iko Mbakara usage is to write Iko Mbakara with consistent spelling rules. If you and I use the same spelling, we understand each other better.

Consistent spelling may be pronounced in different ways in different places. In other words, the spelling of an inclusive Iko Mbakara word does not indicate how to pronounce it. In fact, we believe there is no such thing as correct pronunciation. Rather, we think your pronunciation is correct when you can be understood by other Iko Mbakara speakers.

Sign up to receive updates in your Iko Mbakara at `https://efi.kasahorow.org/subscribe`.

Sharing License

You may freely photocopy and redistribute this book for private or commercial use. No restrictions. Yes go ahead. Do good by sharing.

Errata

All mistakes are ours. When you find one, please let us know so we can fix it.

Please send corrections to help@kasahorow.org.

Modern Iko Mbakara

Modern Iko Mbakara is a written form of Iko Mbakara. It is faster to read. It is also faster to understand. This is because Modern Iko Mbakara has been simplified in the following ways:

1. Modern Iko Mbakara uses the plain alphabet of Iko Mbakara.

2. Modern Iko Mbakara uses only basic word classes: nouns, verbs, and conjunctions.

3. Modern Iko Mbakara uses unique spellings for distinct meanings.

4. Modern Iko Mbakara uses spaces between distinct words in a dictionary.

5. Modern Iko Mbakara uses the active voice only.

This guide is designed to get you up to speed quickly with the Modern Iko Mbakara language. We hope that after getting through it you will be able to read, write and speak basic Iko Mbakara sentences to express the following range of concepts:

1. eti mkpo owo [good person]

2. I ima Efia. [I love Efia.]

3. Kofi dia ko udia. [Kofi ate the food.]

4. Mkpong, Amina di ufok. [Tomorrow, Amina will come home.]

5. Ko akparawa ndien ko nka-iferi yum udia. [The boy and the girl want food.]

For teachers of Iko Mbakara, this guide should provide you a concise outline for getting your new language learners to master the basic structure of the Iko Mbakara language.

Modern Iko Mbakara is a spelling system for Iko Mbakara that uses spaces to make Iko Mbakara easier to read. It is the spelling system used in this book.

Before you jump in ...

In the text, any text marked with * indicates ungrammatical usage. Bolded text can be looked up in the index. The guide attempts to use plain English the first time a concept is explained; in this case the technical term is included in square brackets.

Pronunciations are surrounded by /... / signs.

Written form	a
Spoken form	/a/

English translations are placed in italics in [ ] near their Iko Mbakara renditions.

Let's go!

We hope that this guide will help open up the culture of the Iko Mbakara-speaking peoples all over the world to you!
    Go on and be free in Iko Mbakara!

All the words you need

These are the only words you need to know to understand Modern Iko Mbakara as described in this book.
    Of course, there are many more words in Iko Mbakara. Get the Modern Iko Mbakara Dictionary to learn more Iko Mbakara words!

~ ~ ~

afa eyo *(adj)* modern

eti mkpo *(adj)* good

owo *(nom.2)* person

i *(pro)* I

ima *(act)* love

dia *(act)* eat

ko *(det)* the

udia *(nom.1.2)* food

mkpong *(adv)* tomorrow

di *(act)* come

ufok *(nom.1.2)* home

akparawa *(nom.1.2)* boy

nka-iferi *(nom.1.2)* girl

yum *(act)* want

Read Modern Iko Mbakara

~ ~ ~

nka-iferi *(nom.1.2)* girl

ebua *(nom.1)* dog

eto *(nom.1.2)* tree

ufok *(nom.1.2)* house

a *(det)* a

ko *(det)* the

eti mkpo *(adj)* good

afia *(adj)* white

kiet *(adj)* one

akaan *(adj)* old

ufa *(adj)* new

abubit *(adj)* black

mmi *(pos)* my

afo *(pos)* your

enye *(pos)* her

nnyin *(pos.1)* our

ake-mfo *(pos)* your

mmo *(pos)* their

enye *(pos)* his

i *(pro)* I

afo *(pro)* you

anye *(pro)* she

anye *(pro)* he

nnyin *(pro)* we

yous *(pro)* you

nmo *(pro)* they

wut *(act)* show

idagha *(nom.1)* position

ini *(nom)* time

mbem-iso *(pre)* before

ntie *(nom)* place

ke *(pre)* on

ke *(pre)* at

verb *(nom)* verb

edinàm *(nom.1)* action

ima *(act)* love

bep *(act)* ask

dia *(act)* eat

ngwong *(act)* drink

di *(act)* come

tie *(act)* sit

mkpong *(adv)* tomorrow

ntie *(nom.1.2)* place

mi *(adv)* here

do *(adv)* there

akparawa *(nom.1.2)* boy

iko *(nom.1)* statement

noono *(act)* give

stop *(nom.1)* information

udia *(nom.1.2)* food

uko *(nom.1)* command

a *(det)* a

tuho *(act)* start

mbeme *(nom.1.2)* question

yene *(act)* get

ntoro *(exc)* yes

iyo *(exc)* no

nsido *(pro)* what

Write Modern Iko Mbakara

Writing and speaking are different. We write with Modern Iko Mbakara spelling. We speak with different voices and accents. Accents are usually tied to places and so you can tell where someone grew up just by their accent!

Spelling

The following spelling conventions are supported by the Iko Mbakara spellchecker available from kasahorow.

Write for comprehension

1. Do not use accents on top of vowels [diacritics]. Instead structure your sentences to avoid ambiguity.

2. Do not use slang or shortened phrases forms. Instead use full forms to make your text easier to read by new readers.

Importing foreign words

This is a 2-stage process. When words are deemed to have made the transition from specialised terminology into popu- lar usage, this process should be applied to revise the spelling of the word accordingly.

1. **Specialised terminology**: Import into Iko Mbakara specialised terminology unlikely to come into popular usage without a change of spelling. This eliminates the possibility of ambiguity for specialists who are already familiar with the term. It is good practice to indicate the origin language of the specialized terminology.

2. **Popular usage terminology**: Phonetically render into Iko Mbakara new words that are in popular usage or likely to come into popular usage. Use the phonetic preference of the largest city where you can find the most Iko Mbakara speakers. When doing so, stick to the pronunciation pattern of the original language. This enables readers who encounter the word for the first time in writing to pronounce the word in a way that will confirm to their ears that it is indeed not an uncommon term.

Punctuation

Words are separated by spaces and other symbols.
These are the most common symbols and their meanings:

.	Shows the end of a statement. Also used to separate the whole number and the fraction components of a decimal number like 1.23
?	Shows the end of a question

!	Shows the end of a command
,	Shows a short pause
:	Shows a longer pause than a comma

~ ~ ~

wet *(act)* write

tang *(act)* speak

ntre *(act)* be

asong *(adj)* different

nnyin *(pro)* we

Speaking Iko Mbakara

This is a guide for how to read and write Iko Mbakara. We include this section to remind you that the best way to learn how to speak Iko Mbakara is by chatting with someone who grew up speaking Iko Mbakara. kasahorow has communities online where you can meet and befriend people who already speak Iko Mbakara.

Search for **Iko Mbakara kasahorow** on the Internet and join a language group.

Remember that written Modern Iko Mbakara is for keeping records in easy to read Iko Mbakara. It is just the beginning of your Iko Mbakara knowledge.

1. So go make a friend who speaks Iko Mbakara.
2. Speak to them only in Iko Mbakara
3. And they speak to you in Iko Mbakara

For reference, here are the sounds of spoken Iko Mbakara

- vowels:
- consonants:

When you have learned the pronunciation of the basic vocabulary in a *Modern Iko Mbakara Dictionary*, you should be able to follow spoken Iko Mbakara. If after memorizing the pronunciation of basic vocabulary you still cannot follow spoken Iko Mbakara, ask your friend to slow down their rate of talking.

At the slower speed, you should be able to pick up enough words to make sense of what they are saying.

The world is waiting for you to speak your first Iko Mbakara sentence with confidence!

~ ~ ~

ufan *(nom.1.2)* friend

iko *(nom.1)* language

atu *(nom.1)* group

dian *(act)* join

vowel *(nom.1)* vowel

consonant *(nom.1)* consonant

Use These Words

You now know the most common sentence patterns in Iko Mbakara. This section provides basic vocabulary to help you expand the range of things you can say.

Simple Pronouns

- i [*I*]
- afo [*you*]
- anye [*she*]
- anye [*he*]
- nnyin [*we*]
- yous [*you*]
- nmo [*they*]

Ownership

- mmi [*my*]
- afo [*your*]

- enye [*her*]
- enye [*his*]
- nnyin [*our*]
- ake-mfo [*your*]
- mmo [*their*]

Nouns

- nka-iferi [*girl*]
- akparawa [*boy*]
- owo [*person*]
- ebua [*dog*]
- unam [*animal*]
- atom [*atom*]
- eto [*tree*]
- ufok [*house*]
- ufok-nwed [*school*]
- udia [*food*]

Adjectives

- eti mkpo [*good*]
- afia [*white*]
- kiet [*one*]
- akaan [*old*]
- ufa [*new*]

Verbs

- ima (ima) [*love (to love)*]
- yum (yum) [*want (to want)*]
- dia (dia) [*eat (to eat)*]
- ngwong (ngwong) [*drink (to drink)*]
- di (di) [*come (to come)*]
- tie (tie) [*sit (to sit)*]

Adverbs

- mfin [*today*]
- mkpong [*tomorrow*]
- mkpong [*yesterday*]
- mi [*here*]
- do [*there*]

Conjunctions

- 1 ndien 2 [*1 and 2*]
- 1 mmi doho 2 [*1 or 2*]

Exclamations

- ntoro [*yes*]
- iyo [*no*]

Basic Ideas

Numbers

The international number system is based on multiples of the number ten [*decimal*].

- 0 - ikpu-ikpu
- 1 - kiet
- 2 - iba
- 3 - ita
- 4 - inang
- 5 - itin
- 6 - itiokeed
- 7 - itia-aba
- 8 - itia-ita

- 9 - usukkiet
- 10 - duop
- 11 - duopekiet
- 12 - duopeba
- 13 - duop ita
- 14 - duopenan
- 15 - efut
- 16 - efutkiet
- 17 - efid-eba
- 18 - efureta
- 19 - efurenan
- 20 - edip
- 21 - edip-ndien-kiet
- 22 - edip-ndien-iba
- 30 - edip-ye-duop
- 40 - aba
- 50 - aba-ye-duop
- 60 - ata
- 70 - ata-ye-duop
- 80 - anaang
- 90 - anan-ye duop

- 100 - kiet ekpad-nniara
- 1000 - kiet ikie
- 1/2 - ubak
- 1/3 - kiet ake ita
- 2/3 - iba ake ita
- 3/20 - ita ake edip

Time

A day has 24 hours. A year has 365 days or 366 days.

- siere [*dawn*]
- ubaha-usen [*morning*]
- uweme-eyo [*afternoon*]
- ndubire [*evening*]
- okoneyo [*night*]

Days of the week

According to the international standard ISO 8601, Monday is the first day of the modern week.

- akpa usen ke udua [*Monday*]
- ayoho usen iba ke udua [*Tuesday*]
- ayoho usen ita ke udua [*Wednesday*]
- usen inang ke udua [*Thursday*]

- ayoho usen ituon ke udua [*Friday*]
- ayoho usen itiokiet ke udua [*Saturday*]
- edere [*Sunday*]

Months of the year

The international year is divided into 12 months.

- Offiong Kiet [*January*]
- Offiong Iba [*February*]
- Offiong Ita [*March*]
- Offiong Inang [*April*]
- akeme inam [*May*]
- offiong itiokeed [*June*]
- Offiong Itiaba [*July*]
- offiong itia-ita [*August*]
- offiong usukkiet [*September*]
- offiong duop [*October*]
- offiong duopkiet [*November*]
- offiong duopeba [*December*]

So, here are some dates.

- ayoho usen ita ke udua. Offiong Ita 6, 1957 [*Wednesday. March 6, 1957*]

- ayoho usen ituon ke udua. Offiong Itiaba 1, 1960 [*Friday. July 1, 1960*]
- akpa usen ke udua. offiong duopkiet 20, 2000 [*Monday. November 20, 2000*]
- ayoho usen iba ke udua. Offiong Kiet 1, 2030 [*Tuesday. January 1, 2030*]

Directions

- ufiin ubok [*left hand*]
- udom ubok [*right hand*]
- di mi [*to come here*]
- kaa do [*to go there*]
- north [*north*]
- south [*south*]
- east [*east*]
- west [*west*]

Food

- udia [*food*]
- mmong [*water*]
- unam [*meat*]
- iyak [*fish*]
- toh [*plant*]

Transport

- enang ukwak [*bicycle*]
- mkpo isang [*car*]
- train [*train*]
- ubom onyong [*aeroplane*]

Colours

- abubit [*black*]
- idaidat [*red*]
- jellow [*yellow*]
- awawa [*green*]
- blue [*blue*]
- afia [*white*]

Family

- ufok emana [*family*]
- ama [*mum*]
- ette [*father*]
- eyin [*kid*]
- akparawa [*boy*]
- nka-iferi [*girl*]
- ayeneka ete, eka awoden [*uncle*]
- awowan eyeneka ete(eka) [*aunt*]

Occupations

- otor iwang [*farmer*]
- ókó-iyak [*fisherman*]
- ukuk udongoh [*nurse*]
- nam nor [*doctor*]
- akpep-nwed [*teacher*]
- awed nwed [*writer*]
- ayem udua [*trader*]
- aku [*priest*]
- obong [*chief*]

Actions

You will frequently use the simple present tense of the verb "to be". We conjugate it here for your convenience.

- i ntre [*I am*]
- afo ntre [*you are*]
- anye ntre [*she is*]
- anye ntre [*he is*]
- mkpo ntre [*it is*]
- nnyin ntre [*we are*]
- yous ntre [*you are*]
- nmo ntre [*they are*]

Here are frequently opposing verbs in the form that you'll find in kasahorow dictionaries.

- di [*come*]
- kaa [*go*]
- dia [*eat*]
- ngwong [*drink*]
- kud [*read*]
- wet [*write*]
- noono [*give*]
- been [*take*]
- nua [*push*]
- dud [*pull*]

Verbs can be modified by adverbs such as *sop*. Here are some examples:

- di sop [*come quickly*]
- kaa sop [*go quickly*]
- dia sop [*eat quickly*]
- ngwong sop [*drink quickly*]
- kud sop [*read quickly*]
- wet sop [*write quickly*]
- noono sop [*give quickly*]
- been sop [*take quickly*]

Write and speak Iko Mbakara!

With your new knowledge and a modern Iko Mbakara dictionary, you should be able to translate modern Iko Mbakara words and read them aloud with the accent your Iko Mbakara friend taught you.

~ ~ ~

i *(pro)* I

afo *(pro)* you

anye *(pro)* she

anye *(pro)* he

nnyin *(pro)* we

yous *(pro)* you

nmo *(pro)* they

mmi *(pos)* my

afo *(pos)* your

enye *(pos)* her

enye *(pos)* his

nnyin *(pos.1)* our

ake-mfo *(pos)* your

mmo *(pos)* their

nka-iferi *(nom.1.2)* girl

akparawa *(nom.1.2)* boy

owo *(nom.2)* person

ebua *(nom.1)* dog

unam *(nom.1.2)* animal

eto *(nom.1.2)* tree

ufok *(nom.1.2)* house

ufok-nwed *(nom.1)* school

udia *(nom.1.2)* food

eti mkpo *(adj)* good

afia *(adj)* white

kiet *(adj)* one

akaan *(adj)* old

ufa *(adj)* new

ima *(act)* love

yum *(act)* want

dia *(act)* eat

ngwong *(act)* drink

di *(act)* come

tie *(act)* sit

mkpong *(adv)* tomorrow

mi *(adv)* here

do *(adv)* there

ntoro *(exc)* yes

iyo *(exc)* no

ikpu-ikpu *(adj)* zero

iba *(adj)* two

ita *(adj)* three

inang *(adj)* four

itin *(adj)* five

itiokeed *(adj)* six

itia-aba *(adj)* seven

itia-ita *(adj)* eight

usukkiet *(adj)* nine

duop *(adj)* ten

duopekiet *(adj)* eleven

duopeba *(adj)* twelve

duop ita *(adj)* thirteen

duopenan *(adj)* fourteen

efut *(adj)* fifteen

efutkiet *(adj)* sixteen

efid-eba *(adj)* seventeen

efureta *(adj)* eighteen

efurenan *(adj)* nineteen

edip *(num)* twenty

kiet *(num)* one

iba *(num)* two

edip-ye-duop *(adj)* thirty

aba *(adj)* forty

aba-ye-duop *(adj)* fifty

ata *(adj)* sixty

ata-ye-duop *(adj)* seventy

anaang *(adj)* eighty

anan-ye duop *(adj)* ninety

ekpad-nniara *(num)* hundred

ikie *(num)* thousand

ubak *(nom.1)* half

edip *(adj)* twenty

ini *(nom.1)* time

a *(det)* a

usen *(nom.1)* day

yene *(act)* have

24 *(num)* 24

ini *(nom.1)* hour

isua *(nom.1)* year

365 *(num)* 365

366 *(num)* 366

siere *(nom.1)* dawn

ubaha-usen *(nom.1)* morning

uweme-eyo *(nom.1)* afternoon

ndubire *(nom.1)* evening

okoneyo *(nom.1)* night

akpa usen ke udua *(nom)* Monday

ayoho usen iba ke udua *(nom)* Tuesday

ayoho usen ita ke udua *(nom)* Wednesday

usen inang ke udua *(nom)* Thursday

ayoho usen ituon ke udua *(nom)* Friday

ayoho usen itiokiet ke udua *(nom)* Saturday

edere *(nom)* Sunday

Offiong Kiet *(nom)* January

Offiong Iba *(nom)* February

akeme inam *(nom)* May

offiong itiokeed *(nom)* June

Offiong Itiaba *(nom)* July

offiong itia-ita *(nom)* August

offiong usukkiet *(nom)* September

offiong duop *(nom)* October

offiong duopkiet *(nom)* November

offiong duopeba *(nom)* December

ufiin *(adj)* left

ubok *(nom.1)* hand

udom *(adj)* right

kaa *(act)* go

north *(nom.1)* north

south *(nom.1)* south

east *(nom.1)* east

west *(nom.1)* west

mmong *(nom.2)* water

unam *(nom.1)* meat

iyak *(nom.1)* fish

toh *(nom.1)* plant

enang ukwak *(nom.1)* bicycle

mkpo isang *(nom.1.2)* car

train *(nom.1)* train

ubom onyong *(nom.1.2)* aeroplane

abubit *(adj)* black

idaidat *(adj)* red

jellow *(adj)* yellow

awawa *(adj)* green

blue *(adj)* blue

ufok emana *(nom.1.2)* family

ama *(nom.1)* mum

ette *(nom.1.2)* father

eyin *(nom.1.2)* kid

ayeneka ete, eka awoden *(nom.1)* uncle

awowan eyeneka ete(eka) *(nom.2)* aunt

otor iwang *(nom.1)* farmer

ókó-iyak *(nom.1)* fisherman

ukuk udongoh *(nom.1)* nurse

nam nor *(nom.1)* doctor

akpep-nwed *(nom.1)* teacher

awed nwed *(nom.1)* writer

ayem udua *(nom.1)* trader

aku *(nom.1)* priest

obong *(nom.1)* chief

ntre *(act)* be

mkpo *(pro)* it

kud *(act)* read

wet *(act)* write

noono *(act)* give

been *(act)* take

nua *(act)* push

dud *(act)* pull

Basic Iko Mbakara Reading

Read and translate this Iko Mbakara poem.

Ibuot, Afara, Edong Ndien Ukot

Ibuot, afara, edong ndien ukot.
Ibuot, afara, edong ndien ukot.

Eyen, utong, ibuo ndien inua.

Ibuot, afara, edong ndien ukot.
Edong ndien ukot.

    Well done! Thank you!

~ ~ ~

kud *(act)* read

enyem *(det)* this

poem *(nom.1)* poem

ibuot *(nom.1)* head

afara *(nom.1)* shoulder

edong *(nom.1)* knee

ukot *(nom.1)* toe

utong *(nom.1)* ear

ibuo *(nom.1)* nose

inua *(nom.1)* mouth

afo *(exc)* thank you

Basic Iko Mbakara Phrases

Remember these handy phrases to get you out of a tight spot.

Greetings

- aloo [hello]
- emedi [welcome]
- I ntre a akpep-nwed. [I am a teacher.]
- ka di [goodbye]

Respect

- afo [thank you]
- mbok [please]
- kpe [sorry]

Request

- Afo eyin ntre nsido? [What is your name?]
- Aye ntre nsido? [What is that?]

Answer

- ntoro [yes]
- iyo [no]

~ ~ ~

aloo *(exc)* hello

emedi *(exc)* welcome

i *(pro)* I

ntre *(act)* be

a *(det)* a

akpep-nwed *(nom.1)* teacher

ka di *(exc)* goodbye

afo *(exc)* thank you

mbok *(adv)* please

kpe *(exc)* sorry

afo *(pos)* your

eyin *(nom.1.2)* name

nsido *(pro)* what

aye *(det)* that

ntoro *(exc)* yes

iyo *(exc)* no

Basic Iko Mbakara Translation

Kapa [Kw:Efi] ndien afo kpem [Kw:Efi].

1. _____
   afia ufok

2. _____
   i ima Efia

3. _____
   afo ima Efia

4. _____
   anye ima Efia

5. _____
   nnyin ima Efia

6. _____
   yous ima Efia

7. _____
   nmo ima Efia

8. _____
   i dia ko udia

9. _____
   afo dia ko udia

10. _____
    anye dia ko udia

11. _____
    anye dia ko udia

12. _____
    i dia ko udia

13. _____
    nnyin dia ko udia

14. _____
    yous dia ko udia

15. _____
    nmo dia ko udia

16. _____
    i di ufok, mkpong

17. _____
    afo di ufok, mkpong

18. _____
    anye di ufok, mkpong

19. _____
    anye di ufok, mkpong

20. _____
    mkpo di ufok, mkpong

21. _____
    nnyin di ufok, mkpong

22. _____
    yous di ufok, mkpong

23. _____
    nmo di ufok, mkpong

24. _____
    afo ndien i

25. _____
    afo ndien i kud

26. _____
    afo ndien i kud sop

27. _____
    afo ndien i kud a nwéd

28. _____
    afo ndien i kud sop a nwéd

29. _____
    i ntre a eti mkpo owo

30. _____
    afo ntre a eti mkpo owo

31. _____
    Efia ntre a eti mkpo owo

~ ~ ~

afo *(pro)* you

kpem *(act)* learn

afia *(adj)* white

ufok *(nom.1.2)* house

i *(pro)* I

ima *(act)* love

anye *(pro)* he

nnyin *(pro)* we

yous *(pro)* you

nmo *(pro)* they

dia *(act)* eat

ko *(det)* the

udia *(nom.1.2)* food

anye *(pro)* she

di *(act)* come

ufok *(nom.1.2)* home

mkpong *(adv)* tomorrow

mkpo *(pro)* it

kud *(act)* read

a *(det)* a

nwéd *(nom.1.2)* book

ntre *(act)* be

eti mkpo *(adj)* good

owo *(nom.2)* person

[Kw:Efi]-English

a b c d e f g h i j k l m n o ọ ó p q r s t u v w x y z

a *(ph)* a

a *(det)* a

aba *(adj)* forty

aba-ye-duop *(adj)* fifty

abaak *(adj)* young

abagha *(pre)* about

abai *(nom.1)* pillar

Abasi *(nom.1)* God

Eyin-obong *(din.1)* Jesus

abiara *(adj)* inactive

abiong *(nom.1)* hunger

abogho *(pre)* above

aboikpa *(nom.1)* lady

abu *(nom.1)* shrimp

abubit *(adj)* black

abung owo-esit *(nom.1)* heart-breaker

accident *(nom.1)* accident

acidic *(adj)* acidic

Acusa *(nom.1)* Hausa

ada iwud *(nom.1)* manager

ada ukara *(nom.1)* leadership

ada ukara *(nom.1)* president

ada ukara *(nom.1)* government

ada-ibout *(nom.1)* leader

ada-ibout *(nom.1)* administration

ada-usung *(nom.1)* director

adan *(nom.1)* grease

adan *(nom.1)* oil

adan-akuok *(nom.1)* honey

adanga *(nom.1)* boundary

adanga *(nom.1)* boundary

adap-mkpo *(nom.1)* customer

address *(nom.1)* address

ademe *(nom.1)* ademe

adiọk *(adj)* dangerous

adjective *(nom.1)* adjective

ado *(adv)* just

ado-ekamba *(act)* be big

adoption *(nom.1)* adoption

adua *(nom.1)* squirrel

aduk *(nom.1)* trumpet

aduma *(nom.1)* thunder

aduñ *(nom.1)* root

adunwan *(act)* yawn

aduuk *(nom.1)* kind

adverb *(nom.1)* adverb

advertisement *(nom.1)* advertisement

afa eyo *(adj)* modern

afa-owo *(nom.1)* novice

afai *(nom.1)* violence

afang *(nom.1)* space

afara *(nom.1)* shoulder

afed *(pro)* us

afed *(adj)* total

afed *(adj)* all

afed *(adj)* whole

afed *(adj)* entire

afed-ini *(adv)* always

afem *(adj)* windy

affair *(nom.1)* affair

Afghanistan *(nom.1)* Afghanistan

afia *(adj)* white

afia *(nom.1)* fairness

afim *(nom.1)* wind

afim *(nom.1)* air

afim – akapa-iko

afiom *(nom.1)* alligator

afit *(act)* shit

afit *(det)* all

afit *(pro)* all

afit-itie *(pro)* everywhere

afo *(pos)* your

afo *(pro)* you

afo *(pro)* your

afo *(exc)* thank you

afon *(adj)* well

afon *(nom.1)* well

afon *(adj)* fine

afon *(adj)* better

afon-akem *(adj)* adequate

afong *(nom.1)* khakhi

african *(adj)* African

aim *(nom.1)* objective

Ajoa *(nom.1)* Ajoa

akaan *(adj)* old

akaba owo *(nom.1)* adult

akai *(nom.1)* forest

akam *(act)* pray

akam *(nom.1)* prayer

akamba *(adj)* big

akamba *(adj)* large

akamba *(adj)* huge

akan *(cjn)* than

akan *(adj)* previous

akan *(kw.1)* Akan

akan-awan *(nom.1)* old lady

akan-eden *(nom.1)* old man

akapa-iko *(nom.1)* translator

ake ake *(pre)* of

ake-mfo *(pos)* your

ake-mfo *(pro)* yours

akeb keb *(nom.1)* lightning

akem *(act)* fulfill

akeme afum akeme afum *(nom.1.2)* airconditioner

akeme ido *(adv)* maybe

computer akeme iko *(nom.1.2)* computer

akeme inam *(nom.1)* May

ekebe ndise akeme ndise *(nom.1.2)* television

ekebe uting iko akeme uting iko *(nom.1.2)* radio

akid-nkikid *(nom.1)* prophet

akikere *(nom.1)* thought

akong eto akong eto *(nom.1.2)* carpenter

akoñko *(nom.1)* hero

akpa *(nom.1)* sea

akpa *(adj)* dead

akpa *(nom.1)* first

akpa *(adj)* first

akpa *(nom.1)* ocean

akpa usen ke udua akpa usen ke udua *(nom.1.2)* Monday

akpa-eyen *(nom.1)* firstborn

akpa-isong *(nom.1)* ant

akpa-mfia *(nom.1)* leprosy

akpa-owo *(nom.1)* pioneer

akpaikpai-ikọng *(nom.1)* tuberculosis

akpakara *(nom.1)* bench

akpan mkpo *(adj)* essential

akpan mkpo *(nom.1)* impact

akpan mkpo *(adj)* major

akpan mkpo *(adj)* important

akpan mkpo *(adj)* solemn

akpaniko *(nom.1)* truth

akpaniko *(adj)* true

akpara *(nom.1)* philanderer

akpara *(nom.1)* flirting

akpara *(nom.1)* slut

akparawa eden *(nom.1.2)* boy

akpasa *(nom.1)* basket

akpatere *(act)* end

akpatere *(nom.1)* end

akpatire *(adj)* last

akpatire *(nom.1)* conclusion

akpe-do *(cjn)* if

akpe-ikpe *(nom.1)* lawyer

akpeme ufok akpeme ufok *(nom.1.2)* housekeeper

akpeme-itie *(nom.1)* security

akpep-nwed *(nom.1)* teacher

akpep-utom *(nom.1)* apprentice

akpo *(nom.1)* bone

akpo asak-edem *(nom.1)* spine

akpo-mmong *(nom.1)* bucket

akpo-mmong *(nom.1)* pail

akpo-owo *(nom.1)* corpse

akpor *(nom.1)* pipe

akpotiod akpotiod *(nom.1.2)* authority

aku *(nom.1)* priest

akum *(adj)* allergic

akuọk *(nom.1)* bee

akwa *(nom.1)* Almighty

akwa *(adj)* almighty

Akwa anwa mbre *(nom.1)* stadium

algebra *(nom.1)* algebra

algorithm *(nom.1)* algorithm

aloo *(exc)* hello

aluminum *(sci)* aluminum

Ama *(nom.1)* Ama

ama *(nom.1)* mum

ama-iban *(nom.1)* cheater

amana iba *(nom.2)* twin

amem *(adj)* flexible

amen *(exc)* amen

americium *(sci)* americium

ami *(pro)* me

amia-ibit *(nom.1)* drummer

anaang *(adj)* eighty

anam-utom *(nom.1)* worker

anan *(act)* rear

anan-ye duop *(adj)* ninety

andibip *(nom.1)* requester

andibod *(nom.2)* maker

andidep *(nom.1)* buyer

andikama *(nom.1)* user

andikan *(nom.1)* champion

andikara *(nom.1)* management

andinọọ *(nom.1)* giver

andiwam *(nom.1)* sponsor

andiwam *(nom.1)* saviour

aneke-akpon *(act)* overgrow

aneke-yoho *(act)* overflow

anen ita *(nom.1)* triangle

angel *(nom.1)* angel

anie *(pro)* whose

anie owo *(pro)* who

aniong *(act)* be lengthy

anise anise *(nom.1.10)* anise

aniseed *(nom.1)* aniseed

antelope *(nom.1)* antelope

antimony *(sci)* antimony

anvil *(nom.1)* anvil

anwa *(nom.1)* cat

anwanga *(act)* understand

anya anya anya-anya *(nom.1.2)* crown

anyan *(adj)* straight

anye *(pro)* that

anye *(pro)* her

anye *(pro)* he

anye *(pro)* him

anye *(pos)* its

anye *(pro)* she

anye *(pre)* that

apple *(nom.1)* apple

Arabiya *(nom.1)* Arabic

argon *(sci)* argon

arithmetic *(nom.1)* arithmetic

arsenic *(sci)* arsenic

art *(nom.1)* art

asaha-saha *(adj)* special

asana *(act)* tidy

asana *(nom.1)* potty

asanga *(adj)* distinguished

asanga-edem *(nom.1)* lastborn

asangasanga *(adj)* divine

asara-ikpang *(nom.1)* fork

asen *(nom.1)* stranger

asere *(adj)* unkempt

asio-mbere *(nom.1)* actress

asip asip *(nom.1.2)* artery

osio mbere asip *(nom.1.2)* artist

asip *(adj)* thin

asip *(nom.1)* vein

asoho *(adv)* still

asong *(adj)* different

asong *(adj)* difficult

asong *(adv)* hard

astatine *(sci)* astatine

ata *(adj)* sixty

ata *(adj)* actual

ata amor *(adj)* main

ata ifiok *(nom.1)* graduate

ata utop ata utop *(nom.1.2)* hunter

ata-ye-duop *(adj)* seventy

ataa *(nom.1)* reality

ataa *(adj)* real

ataat *(nom.1)* wasp

atak-tak *(nom.1)* grasshopper

atayat *(nom.10)* hut

atlantic *(adj)* Atlantic

atom *(sci)* atom

atongho *(adj)* deep

atu *(nom.1)* jar

atu *(nom.1)* group

australia *(nom.1)* Australia

autumn *(nom.1)* Autumn

awaha *(adv)* obviously

awak *(adj)* more

awan *(nom.2)* wife

awan akpa *(nom.2)* widower

awangha *(adv)* clearly

awawa *(adj)* green

awed nwed *(nom.1)* writer

awesome *(adj)* awesome

awo *(nom.1)* being

awo *(nom.1)* humankind

awoden *(nom.1)* male

awoden *(nom.1)* man

awowan *(adj)* female

nka-iferi awowan *(nom.1.2)* girl

awowan *(nom.1)* female

awowan eyeneka ete(eka) *(nom.2)* aunt

awung-kpa *(act)* be drunk

ayaiya *(adj)* beautiful

ayam-udua *(nom.1)* seller

aye *(det)* that

aye *(exc)* aye

aye *(cjn)* that

ayem udua *(nom.1)* trader

ayen awoden ayeneka ete,eka *(nom.1)* nephew

ayen awowan ayeneka ete,eka *(nom.1)* niece

ayen ayeneka ete ayen eyeneka ete(eka) *(nom.1.2)* cousin

ayen ebe ayen ebe (awan) *(nom.1.2)* step-child

eyeneka owoden ayeneka awoden *(nom.1.2)* brother

eyeneka-awowan ayeneka awowan *(nom.1.2)* sister

ayeneka ete ayeneka ete,eka awowan *(nom.1.10)* auntie

ayeneka ete,eka awoden *(nom.1)* uncle

ayeyen *(nom.2)* grandchild

ayeyen ayeyen *(nom.1.2)* granddaughter

ayeyen ayeyen *(nom.1.2)* grandson

ayin awoden *(nom.2)* son

ayin awowan *(nom.2)* daughter

ayin-ọbọng *(nom.1)* prince

eyin aying *(nom.1.2)* name

ayio *(nom.1)* weather

ayoho *(adj)* full

ayoho usen iba ke udua *(nom.1)* Tuesday

ayoho usen ita ke udua *(nom.2)* Wednesday

ayoho usen itiokiet ke udua *(nom.1)* Saturday

ayoho usen ituon ke udua *(nom.2)* Friday

ayoyo *(nom.1)* ayoyo

azonto *(nom.1)* azonto

b *(ph)* b

ba *(act)* reign

ba-afon *(act)* be good

baak *(act)* fear

baanga *(act)* gossip

baanga *(nom.1)* division

backlog *(nom.1)* backlog

bak *(adj)* early

bak *(adj)* cheap

bambara *(nom.1)* Bambara

ban *(act)* sharpen

ban *(nom.1)* saucepan

banker *(nom.1)* banker

barium *(sci)* barium

barrel *(nom.1)* barrel

basketball *(nom.1)* basketball

bat *(act)* count

beach *(nom.1)* beach

beaker *(nom.1)* beaker

bed *(act)* remain

bed *(act)* close

been *(act)* take

been *(nom.1)* pick

beenge *(nom.1)* preparation

beenge *(nom.1)* preparations

beenge *(act)* beg

beenge *(act)* prepare

bekke *(act)* belch

bem *(act)* protect

bem *(nom.1)* watch

bem *(act)* watch

bemba *(kw.1)* Bemba

ben-di *(act)* bring

bep *(act)* ask

bere *(act)* lean on

berkelium *(sci)* berkelium

beryllium *(sci)* beryllium

besin *(nom.1)* basin

bet *(act)* wait

beud beud *(nom.1.2)* shyness

bia *(nom.1)* yam

bia *(act)* betray

biad *(act)* defile

biad *(act)* sabotage

biad *(act)* ruin

biad *(act)* spend

biad *(nom.1)* spending

biak *(adj)* painful

biangha *(nom.1)* treason

biara *(nom.1)* decay

biara *(act)* spoil

biat *(act)* disappoint

biere *(act)* stop

biet *(act)* resemble

biine *(act)* chase

bile *(nom.1)* bile

bill *(nom.1)* bill

biong *(adj)* hungry

bip *(act)* request

bire *(act)* play

bismuth *(sci)* bismuth

bit *(act)* lay

biyo *(act)* pass by

biyo *(act)* pass

blacksmith *(nom.1)* blacksmith

blog *(nom.1)* blog

blue *(adj)* blue

bo *(act)* accept

bo *(act)* collect

bọ *(nom.1)* acceptance

bó *(act)* receive

bobo *(nom.1)* pawpaw

bod *(act)* create

bod *(nom.1)* creation

bohrium *(sci)* bohrium

boi *(nom.1)* collection

bolom-bolom *(nom.1)* balloon

bom *(act)* break

bomb *(nom.1)* bomb

bong *(act)* scream

bong *(act)* yell

book *(act)* pacify

bop *(act)* tie

bop *(nom.1)* tie

boro *(act)* respond

boron *(sci)* boron

bracket *(nom.1)* bracket

bromine *(sci)* bromine

brown *(adj)* brown

buffer *(nom.1)* buffer

buto *(act)* rot

butter *(nom.1)* butter

button *(nom.1)* button

buut *(act)* shame

buut *(nom.1)* shame

by *(pre)* by

cabbage *(nom.1)* cabbage

cadmium *(sci)* cadmium

caesium *(sci)* caesium

cake *(nom.1)* cake

calcium *(sci)* calcium

calculus *(nom.1)* calculus

californium *(sci)* californium

Cameroon *(nom.1)* Cameroon

camp *(nom.1)* camp

canada *(nom.1)* Canada

capital *(nom.1)* capital

carbon *(sci)* carbon

card *(nom.1)* card

carrot *(nom.1)* carrot

cartoon *(nom.1)* cartoon

cast *(nom.1)* cast

castle *(nom.1)* castle

cedi *(nom.1)* cedi

cerium *(sci)* cerium

certificate *(nom.1)* degree

characteristic *(adj)* characteristic

chariot *(nom.1)* chariot

cheese *(nom.1)* cheese

chemistry *(nom.1)* chemistry

Chewa Chewa *(kw.1.2)* Chewa

chlorine *(sci)* chlorine

chocolate *(nom.1)* chocolate

chromium *(sci)* chromium

cilantro *(nom.1)* cilantro

clarion *(adj)* clarion

cloud-computing *(nom.1)* cloud computing

coat *(nom.1)* coat

cobalt *(sci)* cobalt

cocoa *(nom.1)* cocoa

compound-interest *(nom.1)* compound interest

computing *(nom.1)* computing

congenial *(adj)* congenial

Congo-Brazzaville *(nom.1)* Congo-Brazzaville

conjunction *(nom.1)* conjunction

conscience *(nom.1)* conscience

consonant *(nom.1)* consonant

constituency *(nom.1)* constituency

contract *(nom.1)* contract

coop *(nom.1)* coop

cooperation *(nom.1)* cooperation

copper *(sci)* copper

creativity *(nom.1)* creativity

curium *(sci)* curium

d *(ph)* d

da *(act)* stand

daara *(act)* rejoice

daara *(adj)* merry

daat *(act)* ripen

daha *(act)* forgive

daka *(nom.1)* travel

dakada *(act)* raise

dakka *(act)* travel

dam *(nom.1)* dam

danga *(act)* book

dapa *(act)* dream

dara *(act)* exult

darmstadtium *(sci)* darmstadtium

data *(nom.1)* data

deb *(act)* purchase

deb *(act)* buy

deeme *(act)* share

deeng *(act)* sink

deghe *(act)* cool

deme *(act)* revive

deme *(act)* wake up

democracy *(nom.1)* democracy

deposit *(act)* deposit

depth *(nom.1)* depth

design *(nom.1)* design

device *(nom.1)* device

di *(nom.1)* coming

di *(act)* come

dia *(act)* eat

dia-sop *(act)* devour

dian *(act)* stamp

dian *(act)* paste

dian *(nom.1)* multiplication

dian *(act)* integrate

dian *(act)* add

dian *(act)* join

dian *(act)* combine

diana *(act)* unite

diana *(nom.1)* unity

diana-kiet *(nom.1)* union

diana-kiet *(adv)* together

diangare *(act)* choose

dibe *(act)* hide

die *(adv)* how

dienne *(adj)* disgusting

dioho *(act)* predict

dioho-die *(nom.1)* technology

diok *(adj)* bad

diong *(act)* repair

diong *(nom.1)* repair

diongho *(adj)* familiar

diongho- mkpo *(adj)* smart

do *(nom.1)* there

do *(act)* wed

do *(act)* become

do *(adv)* there

do-akpatere *(act)* be last

dob *(adj)* quiet

dobo *(adj)* silent

document *(nom.1)*document

dod-eyen *(nom.1)* independence

doho *(act)* tell

doho *(nom.1)* report

dok *(act)* weave

dok *(act)* dig

dokko yaha mkpo-aba *(nom.1)* description

dokko yaha-aba *(adj)* descriptive

dollar *(nom.1)* dollar

domo *(act)* switch on

domo *(act)* test

domo *(act)* weigh

domo *(act)* measure

dong *(act)* send

dong *(act)* tease

dong *(act)* stay

dono *(act)* smoothen

dot *(act)* befit

doughnut *(nom.1)* doughnut

downward *(adv)* downward

drama *(nom.1)* drama

du *(adj)* living

duak *(act)* wish

dubnium *(sci)* dubnium

dud *(act)* pull

dud *(adj)* striped

dud ayen *(adj)* dependable

due *(act)* live

due *(act)* miss

due *(act)* err

duk *(act)* enter

duk-udod *(act)* rest

dukpo *(adj)* busy

duo *(act)* stumble

duo *(act)* fall

duoi *(act)* pour

duook *(act)* lose

duop *(adj)* ten

duop enaang *(adj)* fourteenth

duop ita *(adj)* thirteen

duop ita *(adj)* thirteenth

duop-o-kiet *(adj)* eleventh

duopeba *(adj)* twelve

duopekiet *(adj)* eleven

duopenan *(adj)* fourteen

dut *(act)* draw

DVD *(nom.1)* DVD

dwe *(nom.1)* sin

dwe *(adv)* wrongly

dwe *(adj)* wrong

dysprosium *(sci)* dysprosium

e *(ph)* ay

earthenware *(nom.1)* earthenware

earthquake *(nom.1)* quake

east *(nom.1)* east

east-timor *(nom.1)* East Timor

eastern *(adj)* eastern

eba *(nom.1)* second

eba *(nom.1)* breast

ebe ebe *(nom.1.2)* husband

ebe ebe(awan) *(nom.1.2)* spouse

ebe awan ebe awan *(nom.1.2)* stepfather

ebe kpa *(nom.2)* widow

ebe-kpa *(adj)* widowed

ebet *(nom.1)* deer

ebiet unam udia ufok utem mkpo *(nom.1.2)* kitchen

ebikpod *(nom.1)* maize

ebok *(nom.1)* monkey

ebot *(nom.1)* goat

ebua *(nom.1)* dog

ebup *(nom.1)* bridge

economy *(nom.1)* economy

edak *(nom.1)* loin

edak edak *(nom.1.2)* abdomen

eded *(nom.1)* tooth

edem *(nom.1)* back

edem-esa *(nom.1)* backyard

edem-eyong *(nom.1)* heaven

edem-ibuot *(nom.1)* back of the head

edeme *(nom.1)* tongue

eden owo *(adj)* male

edere *(nom.1)* Sunday

edere *(nom.1)* service

edesi *(nom.1)* rice

edi *(nom.1)* pig

edidem *(nom.1)* king

edidiọng *(nom.1)* blessing

edien *(cjn)* if ... then

edikan *(act)* forbid

edim *(nom.1)* rain

edim *(adj)* rainy

edima *(nom.1)* beloved

edinàm *(nom.1)* action

edinam *(nom.1)* programme

edinam *(nom.1)* project

edinam *(nom.1)* act

edinam *(nom.1)* activity

edinam *(nom.1)* event

edip *(adj)* twenty

edip-mme-duop *(adj)* thirtieth

edip-ye-duop *(adj)* thirty

edisana *(adj)* holy

edisat *(nom.1)* comb

editibe *(nom.1)* vaccine

editongo editongo *(nom.1.2)* beginning

editongo *(nom.1)* introduction

edong *(nom.1)* knee

edong *(nom.1)* sheep

edu *(nom.1)* character

edu owo *(nom.1)* habit

edu-unam mkpo *(nom.1)* manner

eduat *(nom.1)* spear

efak *(nom.1)* district

efak *(nom.1)* community

efak *(act)* serve

efen *(adj)* other

efen *(adj)* another

efen *(adj)* next

efere *(nom.1)* soup

efere *(nom.1)* stew

efere-abak *(nom.1)* palmnut soup

efficiency *(nom.1)* efficiency

effiom *(nom.1)* crocodile

efiat *(nom.1)* kola nut

efid *(adj)* fifteenth

efid eta *(adj)* eighteenth

efid-eba *(adj)* seventeen

efurenan *(adj)* nineteen

efureta *(adj)* eighteen

efut *(adj)* fifteen

efutkiet *(adj)* sixteenth

efutkiet *(adj)* sixteen

einsteinium *(sci)* einsteinium

eka *(nom.1)* mom

eka esit ubok *(nom.1)* palm

eka ufok *(nom.2)* madam

ekam *(nom.2)* grandmother

ekamba *(adj)* maximum

ekamba *(adj)* massive

owo uwan ekamba awowan *(nom.1.2)* woman

ekamba owo *(adj)* elder

ekamba owo *(nom.1)* elder

ekarika *(nom.1)* snow

ekarika *(adj)* snowy

ekarika *(nom.1)* harmattan

ekarika *(nom.1)* winter

eke mi *(pro)* mine

ekebe ntuhube *(nom.1)* refrigerator

ekeme *(nom.1)* box

ekikere ke baha owo *(nom.1)* reputation

ekim *(nom.1)* darkness

ekom *(act)* praise

ekom *(nom.1)* salutation

ekom *(nom.1)* praise

ekom *(nom.1)* walnut

ekom *(act)* appreciate

ekom *(exc)* condolences

ekom *(nom.1)* greeting

ekom *(nom.1)* gratitude

ekong *(nom.1)* battle

ekong *(act)* battle

ekong *(nom.1)* war

ekong ubok *(nom.1)* elbow

ekop *(nom.1)* navel

ekop *(nom.1)* umbilicus

ekpad-nniara *(adj)* hundred

ekpang *(nom.1)* spatula

ekpat *(nom.1)* bag

ekpat ofong *(nom.1)* cushion

ekpe *(nom.1)* lion

ekpe-udia *(nom.1)* glutton

ekpeme *(nom.1)* bottle

ekpo mfem *(nom.1)* ringworm

ekpoh *(nom.1)* mouse

ekpok *(nom.1)* lizard

ekpri *(adv)* a little

ekpri *(adj)* small

ekpri *(nom.1)* little

ekpri *(adj)* minimum

eyin ekpri eyen *(nom.1.2)* kid

ekpri-mkpọ *(nom.1)* mouthful

ekpu *(nom.1)* rat

eku mbakara *(nom.1)* rabbit

Ekua *(nom.1)* Ekua

ekwod *(nom.1)* frog

ekwod-mmong *(nom.1)* turtle

ekwong *(nom.1)* snail

election *(nom.1)* election

electron *(sci)* electron

element *(sci.1)* element

ellinika *(nom.1)* Modern Greek

email *(nom.1)* email

man *(act)* birth

emana *(nom.1)* birth

emana *(nom.1)* generation

Emana-abasi *(nom.1)* Christmas

emancipator *(nom.1)* emancipator

emedi *(exc)* welcome

emem *(nom.1)* peace

emesiere *(exc)* good morning

Emmanuel *(din.1)* Emmanuel

enang *(nom.1)* cow

enang *(nom.1)* horse

enang *(nom.1)* ox

enang mbiomo *(nom.1)* donkey

enang ukwak *(nom.1)* bicycle

England *(nom.1)* England

eniang mbiomo *(nom.1)* camel

enin *(nom.1)* elephant

eno *(nom.1)* award

eno *(nom.2)* gift

eno-ndongesit *(nom.1)* compensation

enye *(pos)* her

enye *(pos)* his

enyem *(det)* this

epire *(adj)* tiny

erbium *(sci)* erbium

ererimbot *(nom.1)* soil

ererimbot *(nom.1)* planet

ererimbot *(nom.1)* world

eriyaha *(nom.1)* salvation

esa *(nom.1)* verandah

esen *(adj)* strange

eset *(adj)* ancient

eset *(nom.1)* ancient times

esio *(nom.1)* pot

esion *(nom.1)* outside

esion *(adv)* outside

esit *(nom.1)* heart

esit *(nom.1)* chest

esit *(nom.2)* mind

esit-mbom *(nom.1)* empathy

esop *(nom.1)* court

esuk *(nom.1)* harbour

esuo-uframkpo *(nom.1)* pan

ete ebe ette ebe(awan) *(nom.1.2)* father-in-law

ete ye eka ette ye eka *(nom.1.2)* parent

ete/eka ufok *(nom.1)* boss

etebom *(nom.2)* grandpa

etetighe *(nom.1)* heel

eti *(nom.1)* good

eti *(nom.1)* goodness

eti *(adj)* excellent

eti *(nom.1)* virtue

eti *(adj)* nice

eti mkpo oti mkpo *(nom.1.2)* quality

eti mkpo *(adj)* good

eti-ido *(adj)* friendly

eti-utom *(exc)* good job

eti-uwem *(nom.1)* honesty

eti-uwem *(nom.1)* generosity

etido *(nom.1)* kindness

etido *(adj)* kind

etiero *(exc)* good afternoon

etike *(nom.1)* okro

eto *(nom.1)* stick

eto *(nom.1)* wood

eto eto *(nom.1.2)* tree

eto nwed *(nom.1)* pen

eto nwed *(nom.1)* chalk

eto uwed nwed *(nom.1)* pencil

eto-bed *(nom.1)* bedstead

etop *(nom.1)* message

etop *(nom.2)* news

ette ette *(nom.1.2)* father

mme usor usor ette ette *(nom.1.2)* ancestor

ette ye eka *(act)* parent

etubom *(nom.1)* pastor

etuk-akpok *(nom.1)* gecko

europe *(nom.1)* Europe

europium *(sci)* europium

Evegbe *(kw.1)* Gbe

ewongho *(nom.1)* oath

ewongó *(nom.1)* promise

ewuoot *(act)* loan

ewuoot *(nom.1)* loan

executioner *(nom.1)* executioner

eye *(pro)* herself

eye *(pro)* himself

eye-adok-usop *(exc)* that escalated quickly

eyeke *(det)* which

eyem *(pro)* this

eyem *(pro)* these

eyen *(nom.1)* eye

eyen-mkpo *(nom.1)* shade

eyen-mkpo *(act)* colour

eyen-ufok *(nom.1)* maid

eyen-ufoknwed *(nom.1)* student

eyin-eka *(nom.1)* relative

eyong *(adv)* up

eyong okom eyong okom *(nom.1.2)* roof

f *(ph)* f

faanga *(act)* litigate

faanga *(nom.1)* argument

faanga *(act)* argue

faap *(act)* climb

fad *(act)* embrace

fad *(nom.1)* hug

fana *(act)* hassle

fana *(act)* harass

fana *(nom.1)* worry

feghe *(act)* run

feghe *(act)* flee

fermium *(sci)* fermium

fiak *(act)* twist

fiak *(adv)* again

fiak-nam *(act)* repeat

fiim *(act)* shrink

fiip *(act)* suckle

fiip *(act)* suck

fik *(act)* press

fik *(act)* click

fik-ubọk *(nom.1)* vote

fim *(nom.1)* wave

fino *(nom.1)* bother

fiok *(act)* know

fiomo *(act)* bully

fip fip *(nom.1.2)* sock

fire *(act)* forget

fishing-net *(nom.1)* fishing-net

fit *(act)* blow

fịt-bọọt *(nom.1)* football

flag *(nom.1)* flag

fluorine *(sci)* fluorine

fop *(adj)* blazing

fop *(act)* roast

fop *(act)* burn

forho *(act)* caress

foro *(act)* thrive

fox *(nom.1)* fox

francium *(sci)* francium

frang *(act)* fry

fray *(act)* fray

french *(nom.1)* French

friction *(nom.1)* friction

frighten *(act)* frighten

frightening *(adj)* frightening

fruitful *(adj)* fruitful

fugho *(adj)* sad

fula *(nom.1)* Fula

furo *(act)* fly

furo *(act)* wring

furo *(nom.1)* fly

fut *(act)* fold

fuuk *(act)* cover

fuuro *(adj)* cool

g *(ph)* g

Gadangme *(nom.1)* GaDangme

gadolinium *(sci)* gadolinium

gallium *(sci)* gallium

Gandhi *(din.1)* Gandhi

gari *(nom.1)* gari

gaseous *(adj)* gaseous

geography *(nom.1)* geography

geometry *(nom.1)* geometry

germanium *(sci)* germanium

Germany *(nom.1)* Germany

Ghana *(nom.1)* Ghana

ginger *(nom.1)* ginger

giraffe *(nom.1)* giraffe

global-warming *(nom.1)* global warming

goal *(nom.1)* goal

gold *(sci)* gold

gong-gong *(nom.1)* gong gong

good-evening *(exc)* good evening

grasp *(act)* grasp

groin *(nom.1)* groin

Guinea-Bissau *(nom.1)* Guinea-Bissau

guitar *(nom.1)* guitar

gwod *(act)* extinguish

h *(ph)* h

habitat *(nom.1)* habitat

hafnium *(sci)* hafnium

hallelujah *(exc)* hallelujah

hammer *(nom.1)* hammer

hassium *(sci)* hassium

headphone *(nom.1)* headphone

hedgehog *(nom.1)* hedgehog

helium *(sci)* helium

hi *(exc)* hi

highlife *(nom.1)* highlife

hiplife *(nom.1)* hiplife

holmium *(sci)* holmium

horn *(nom.1)* horn

hydrogen *(sci)* hydrogen

hydrogen *(nom.1)* hydrogen

i *(ph)* ee

i *(pro)* I

i *(nom.1)* Yaa

iba *(adj)* second

iba *(adj)* two

ibaak *(adj)* wicked

ibad *(nom.1)* accounts

ibad *(nom.1)* maths

ibad *(nom.1)* amount

ibad *(nom.1)* accountability

ibad *(nom.1)* account

ibad ibad *(nom.1.2)* accounting

ibad okuk *(nom.1)* sum

ibad-mkpo *(act)* figure

ibad-mkpo *(nom.1)* number

ibad-owo *(nom.1)* population

ibaha-ufǫn *(adj)* unnecessary

ibifik ibifik *(nom.1.2)* breadth

ibikpai *(nom.1)* numbness

ibio *(adj)* short

ibio-iko *(nom.1)* topic

ibiom *(nom.1)* dove

ibit *(nom.1)* drum

ibit-ikwo *(nom.1)* beat

ibok *(nom.1)* injection

ibok *(nom.2)* medicine

iboro iboro *(nom.1.2)* answer

iboró *(nom.1)* solution

iboro *(act)* reply

iboro *(act)* answer

iboro *(nom.1)* response

iboro *(act)* report

iboro *(nom.1)* feedback

resuts *(nom.1)* result

ibuo *(nom.1)* nose

ibuot *(nom.1)* head

ice *(nom.1)* ice

icecream *(nom.1)* ice-cream

idaak *(pre)* under

idaak *(adv)* under

idagha *(nom.1)* position

idagha *(nom.1)* moment

idagha *(nom.1)* height

idaha ke *(adv)* when

idaha-idaha *(adj)* simple

idaidat *(adj)* red

idaidat *(adj)* scarlet

idang idang *(nom.1.2)* arrow

idang *(nom.1)* bow

idap *(act)* doze

idap *(act)* sleep

idap *(nom.1)* drowsiness

idaresit afa isua *(exc)* happy new year

ideal *(adj)* ideal

ided *(nom.1)* hair

idektrik *(nom.1)* electricity

idektronic *(adj)* electronic

idem idem *(nom.1.2)* body

idem *(nom.1)* health

idem mfó *(exc)* how are you

idem mmi osong *(exc)* I am well

idem-mfo *(pro)* yourself

idem-mfo *(pro)* yourselves

idem-mmor *(pro)* themselves

idet-inua *(nom.1)* mustache

idiok *(nom.1)* evil

idiok *(nom.1)* chimpanzee

idiok *(adj)* wild

idiok esit *(nom.1)* jealousy

idiok ufik *(nom.1)* foul

idiok-afum *(nom.1)* pollution

idiok-esit *(nom.1)* ingratitude

idiok-mkpo *(nom.1)* crime

idiok-mkpo *(nom.1)* abomination

idiom *(nom.1)* idiom

idiongho *(act)* signify

idiongho *(nom.1)* symbol

idiongho *(din)* Mark

idiongho *(nom.1)* mark

idip *(nom.1)* stomach

idip *(nom.1)* pregnancy

ido *(nom.1)* policy

ido *(nom.1)* culture

ido ido *(nom.1.2)* behaviour

idob *(adj)* boring

idoho *(det)* not

idoho *(adv)* not

idongesit *(nom.1)* comfort

idorenyin *(nom.1)* hope

idorenyin *(nom.1)* aspiration

idorenyin *(nom.1)* confidence

idung *(nom.1)* village

idwo mmong *(nom.1)* cataract

ifiok *(adj)* civilized

ifiok *(nom.1)* idea

ifiok *(adj)* wise

ifiok *(nom.1)* experience

ifiok *(nom.1)* knowledge

ifiok *(nom.1)* wisdom

ifok *(adj)* intelligent

ifot *(nom.1)* witch

ifot *(nom.1)* witchcraft

ifu *(nom.1)* laziness

ifu *(adj)* lazy

ifum *(nom.1)* seat

nkpo itie ifum *(nom.1.2)* chair

ifum-ukara *(nom.1)* throne

ifuọ *(nom.1)* stool

ifuo *(nom.1)* poop

iguana *(nom.1)* iguana

ikang *(act)* fire

ikang *(nom.1)* gun

ikang *(adj)* electric

ikang *(nom.1)* fire

ike *(nom.1)* tobacco

ikemeke *(adv)* never

ikemke ndibon *(adj)* infertile

ikie *(adj)* thousand

ikim *(nom.1)* urine

iko *(nom.1)* statement

iko *(nom.1)* language

iko *(nom.1)* sentence

iko *(nom.1)* tin

iko *(nom.1)* calabash

iko *(sci)* tin

iko iko *(nom.1.2)* word

iko flower *(nom.1)* vase

iko mbakara *(kw.1)* English

okop iko mmong *(nom.1.2)* cup

iko-abasi *(nom.1)* gospel

iko-ekom *(nom.1)* tribute

ikon *(nom.1)* xylophone

ikon *(nom.1)* melon

ikong *(nom.1)* cough

ikong *(nom.1)* lettuce

ikong *(nom.1)* sputum

ikong *(act)* cough

ikpa *(nom.1)* whip

ikpa *(nom.1)* cane

ikpa enang *(nom.2)* cowhide

ikpa enyong *(act)* cloud

ikpa enyoung *(nom.1)* cloud

ikpa enyoung *(nom.1)* sky

ikpa idem *(nom.1)* skin

ikpa nwed ikpa nwed *(nom.1.2)* page

ikpa nwed *(nom.1)* paper

ikpa ukot *(nom.2)* slippers

ikpaukot ikpa ukot *(nom.1.2)* shoe

ikpa-isin *(nom.1)* belt

ikpang ikpang *(nom.1.2)* spoon

ikpang *(act)* ladle

ikpang *(nom.1)* ladle

ikpat *(nom.1)* foot

ikpe *(nom.1)* justice

ikpong *(nom.1)* cocoyam

ikpong *(adv)* alone

ikpu-ikpu *(nom.1)* circle

ikpu-ikpu *(adj)* zero

ikua *(nom.1)* knife

ikwo *(nom.1)* music

ikwo *(nom.1)* song

ikwo *(nom.1)* chorus

Ilimi *(nom.1)* Ndebele

ima *(act)* love

ima *(nom.1)* love

ima *(nom.1)* affection

imam *(nom.1)* laughter

ime *(nom.1)* patience

immerse *(act)* immerse

immigration *(nom.1)* immigrant

imọ *(adj)* rich

imo *(nom.1)* wealth

imperfection *(nom.1)* imperfection

imuk *(adj)* brief

imuum *(nom.1)* dump

imuum *(adj)* mute

ina *(nom.1)* sex

ina nkan-ubok *(nom.1)* rape

ina-esin *(nom.1)* adultery

ina-nkanubok *(act)* rape

inam *(adj)* funny

inang *(adj)* fourth

inang *(adj)* four

India *(nom.1)* India

Indian *(nom.1)* Indian

indian *(adj)* Indian

indigo *(adj)* indigo

indium *(sci)* indium

inem *(adj)* sweet

inem-udia *(nom.1)* sweet potato

inemesit *(nom.1)* joy

inemesit *(nom.1)* happiness

inemesit usen emana *(exc)* happy birthday

infrastructure *(nom.1)* infrastructure

ini *(nom.1)* time

ini *(nom.1)* period

ini *(nom.1)* minute

ini *(nom.1)* times

ini *(nom.1)* hour

ini uwem *(nom.1)* lifetime

ini-iso *(nom.1)* future

ini-ke *(cjn)* when

ini-mkpo *(nom.1)* timetable

inighe *(nom.1)* sweetheart

inim *(nom.1)* parrot

ino *(nom.1)* thief

ino *(nom.1)* theft

ino mkpo inam *(act)* achieve

inoọk *(adj)* greedy

insect *(nom.1)* insect

internet *(nom.1)* internet

inua *(nom.1)* mouth

inua mmong *(nom.1)* tap

inuen *(nom.1)* hawk

inuen *(nom.1)* falcon

inuen *(act)* hawk

inuen inuen *(nom.1.2)* bird

inung *(nom.1)* salt

invest *(act)* invest

invoice *(nom.1)* invoice

iwang eben esa inwang *(nom.1.2)* garden

inyang *(nom.1)* river

inyene *(nom.1)* investment

inyene ufok *(nom.1)* inheritance

inyene-ifiọk *(nom.1)* prudence

iodine *(sci)* iodine

iPhone *(din)* Iphone

iridium *(sci)* iridium

isang *(nom.10)* stroll

isang *(act)* walk

isang-utom *(nom.1)* messenger

isantim *(nom.1)* hippopotamus

isim *(act)* tail

isim *(nom.1)* tail

isin *(nom.1)* waist

isip *(nom.1)* nut

isip mbakara *(nom.1)* coconut

Islam *(nom.1)* Islam

Islamic *(adj)* Islamic

island *(nom.1)* island

iso *(adj)* advance

iso *(nom.1)* face

isobo *(nom.1)* crab

isobo *(nom.1)* lobster

isong *(nom.1)* land

isong *(act)* land

isong *(nom.1)* floor

isọng *(nom.1)* ground

isong *(adv)* down

isua *(nom.1)* age

isua *(nom.1)* year

isua-duop *(nom.1)* decade

isua-ikie *(nom.1)* century

isung *(nom.1)* debt

ita *(nom.1)* blow

ita *(adj)* three

Italiano *(kw.1)* italiano

itam *(nom.1)* hat

itat *(act)* rock

ite *(pro)* it

item *(nom.1)* advice

itene *(adj)* fat

itia-aba *(adj)* seven

itia-ita *(adj)* eight

itiat *(nom.1)* stone

itiat ubedmkpo *(nom.1)* cornerstone

itie *(nom.1)* location

itie *(nom.1)* part

itie *(nom.1)* venue

itie udia uwem *(nom.1)* hotel

itie ukpep mkpo itie ukpep mkpo *(nom.1.2)* class

itie usin okuk *(nom.1)* bank

itie utom *(nom.1)* company

itie utom *(nom.1)* organization

itie-eyen *(nom.1)* womb

itie-ubokutom *(nom.1)* workshop

itie-udiamkpo *(nom.1)* restaurant

itie-ukodnwed *(nom.1)* library

itie-ukpono *(nom.1)* mosque

itie-usiak-idem *(nom.1)* theatre

itie-usio-iyip *(nom.1)* laboratory

itie-utom *(nom.1)* studio

itin *(adj)* five

itiokeed *(adj)* six

itit *(nom.1)* vagina

itók *(nom.1)* race

itong *(nom.1)* neck

itong *(nom.1)* greed

itong *(nom.1)* throat

itong *(nom.1)* curiosity

itong ofong *(nom.1)* shirt

itong ubok *(nom.1)* wrist

itong ukot *(nom.1)* ankle

itóng-ofong *(nom.1)* bodice

Itsekiri *(kw.1)* Itsekiri

itself *(nom.1)* itself

ivory *(nom.1)* ivory

iwa *(nom.1)* cassava

iwang *(nom.1)* farm

iwat *(adj)* grey

iwod-nwed *(nom.1)* chapter

iwuot *(nom.1)* memory

iya *(exc)* wow

iyak *(act)* fish

iyak *(nom.1)* fish

iyaresit *(adj)* annoying

iyaresit *(nom.1)* anger

iyaresit *(nom.1)* frustration

iyaresit *(nom.1)* resentment

iyaresit *(act)* resent

iyene *(nom.1)* asset

iyene *(nom.1)* property

iyene *(nom.1)* prosperity

iyiip *(nom.1)* blood

iyo *(adj)* no

iyo *(exc)* no

j *(ph)* j

jaguar *(nom.1)* jaguar

jama *(nom.1)* jama

japan *(nom.1)* Japan

Japanese *(nom.1)* Japanese

jellow *(adj)* yellow

Jerusalem *(din.1)* Jerusalem

jewelry *(nom.1)* jewelry

johannesburg *(din.1)* Johannesburg

junction *(nom.1)* junction

just *(pre)* just

just *(adj)* just

k *(ph)* k

ka di *(exc)* goodbye

ka edem *(nom.1)* backspace

ka-di *(nom.1)* bye

ka-iso *(act)* continue

ka-iso *(act)* proceed

kaa *(act)* go

kaanga *(act)* promise

kak *(act)* tire

kak *(nom.1)* tiredness

kama *(act)* keep

kama *(act)* use

kama *(act)* owe

kama *(act)* stir

kama *(nom.1)* use

kama *(nom.1)* usage

kan *(act)* surpass

kan *(act)* triumph

kan *(act)* win

kan *(nom.1)* victory

kang *(act)* deny

kapa *(act)* translate

kapa *(nom.1)* translation

kappa-esit *(act)* repent

kara *(act)* govern

kara *(act)* control

ke *(pre)* for

ke *(pre)* to

ke *(pre)* on

ke *(pre)* in

ke *(pre)* at

ke-se *(act)* visit

keed *(pro)* one

keene *(act)* follow

keere *(act)* think

keere *(act)* memorize

keere *(act)* guess

keere *(nom.1)* thinking

keere-keet keere-keet *(adj)* each

kekpe *(act)* pluck

Kenya *(nom.1)* Kenya

kere *(act)* plan

kere *(nom.1)* plan

kid *(act)* found

kid *(act)* meet

kiet *(adj)* one

kim *(act)* sew

kim *(act)* stab

kim *(act)* inject

kim *(adj)* dark

kindergarten *(nom.1)* kindergarten

kindle *(act)* kindle

kit *(act)* catch

kit *(act)* foresee

ko *(det)* the

kod *(nom.1)* reading

kọfi *(nom.1)* coffee

Kofi *(din.1)* Kofi

koi *(act)* scoop

kok *(act)* vomit

kok *(act)* grind

kokko *(act)* rise

kom *(act)* thank

kom *(act)* glorify

kom *(act)* greet

kọm *(act)* care

kongo *(nom.1)* Kongo

koop *(act)* hang

kọọp *(act)* cup

koot *(nom.1)* growth

koot *(act)* grow

kop *(act)* sense

kop *(act)* sue

kop *(act)* taste

kop *(act)* hear

kop *(act)* listen

kop *(nom.1)* sense

kop *(nom.1)* feeling

kop *(act)* feel

kop-buut *(act)* be shy

koran *(nom.1)* koran

kord *(act)* germinate

kpa *(act)* fade

kpa *(nom.1)* cost

kpa *(act)* die

kpaaba *(adj)* flat

kpaat *(nom.1)* distance

kpagha *(act)* cross

kpan *(nom.1)* warning

kpan *(act)* discipline

kpan *(act)* warn

kpana *(nom.1)* framework

kpappa *(act)* lift

kpappa *(nom.1)* lift

kpe *(act)* pay

kpe *(nom.1)* judge

kpe *(exc)* sorry

kpeep *(nom.1)* study

kpeep *(act)* study

kpeke *(act)* slice

kpem *(act)* learn

kpem *(act)* teach

kpeme *(act)* guide

kpeme *(act)* prevent

kpen *(act)* paint

kpere *(act)* approach

kpi *(act)* cut

kpoho *(nom.1)* change

kpoi *(act)* bark

kpọk *(act)* crow

kpokko *(act)* hit

kpon *(adj)* broad

kpong *(act)* leave

kponno *(adj)* clear

kpono *(act)* worship

kpono *(act)* honour

kpono *(act)* obey

kpono *(nom.1)* respect

kpono *(nom.1)* honour

kpono *(act)* respect

kpono *(nom.1)* dignity

kpono *(nom.1)* worship

kpugho *(nom.1)* exchange

kpuho *(nom.1)* development

kpuho *(act)* transform

kpukpru *(adj)* every

kpukpru owo *(pro)* everyone

kpuut *(act)* gather

krio *(nom.1)* Krio

krypton *(sci)* krypton

kuat *(act)* scrape

kud *(act)* call

kud *(act)* read

kuhore *(act)* clean

kuk *(act)* heal

kuohode *(act)* wipe

kuoi *(act)* peel

kuok *(act)* sweep

kuoro *(act)* preach

kup *(nom.1)* heap

kuppo *(act)* open

nkpo uyet usan kusà *(nom.1.2)* sponge

kutor-kutor *(adj)* diverse

kuuk *(act)* shut

kuuk *(act)* shut down

kwehe *(act)* settle

Kweku *(din)* Kweku

kwo *(act)* sing

kwo *(nom.1)* singing

kwo-jama *(act)* sing jama

l *(ph)* l

lab *(nom.1)* lab

lanthanum *(sci)* lanthanum

lawrencium *(sci)* lawrencium

leather *(nom.1)* leather

ledge *(nom.1)* ledge

lemon *(nom.1)* lemon

length *(nom.1)* length

leopard *(nom.1)* leopard

lesotho *(nom.1)* Lesotho

Likpakpaln *(nom.1)* Konkomba

lily *(nom.1)* lily

limal *(act)* build

line *(nom.1)* line

Lingala *(kw.1)* Lingala

link *(nom.1)* link

lithium lithium *(sci.1)* lithium

liver *(nom.1)* liver

living-room *(nom.1)* living-room

lockdown *(nom.1)* lockdown

log-in *(act)* log in

logo *(nom.1)* logo

Lomwe *(nom.1)* Lomwe

lung *(nom.1)* lung

lutetium *(sci)* lutetium

m *(ph)* m

ma *(nom.1)* lover

ma *(act)* admire

ma *(act)* finish

ma *(nom.1)* treasure

ma *(act)* date

ma *(adv)* like

ma *(act)* like

ma *(pre)* like

ma *(act)* adore

magnesium *(sci)* magnesium

mail *(nom.1)* mail

manganese *(sci)* manganese

manko *(nom.1)* mango

map *(nom.1)* map

marijuana *(nom.1)* marijuana

Matthew *(nom.1)* Matthew

mba *(nom.1)* fatigue

mbad *(nom.1)* clay

mbad *(adj)* filthy

mbai *(nom.1)* wing

mbamba *(nom.1)* scorpion

mbara *(nom.1)* nail

mbat *(adj)* dirty

mbat *(nom.1)* mud

mbed *(nom.1)* law

mbed *(nom.1)* tradition

mbem-iso *(pre)* before

mbeme mbeme *(nom.1.2)* question

mben *(nom.1)* corner

mbere *(nom.1)* game

mbid *(nom.1)* mattress

mbiet *(act)* weed

mbiod *(nom.1)* grass

mbire *(nom.1)* play

mboho *(nom.1)* association

mbok *(nom.1)* history

mbok *(adv)* please

mbók-idung *(nom.1)* neighbourhood

mboko *(nom.1)* sugarcane

mbom *(nom.1)* mercy

mbom *(act)* show ... pity

mbom *(adj)* pitiful

mbon *(adj)* scarce

mbon *(nom.2)* scar

mbon unan *(act)* bruise

mbop-ibuot *(nom.1)* headscarf

mboro *(nom.1)* banana

mbot *(nom.1)* porridge

mbri ikpa mbra ikpa *(nom.1.2)* ball

mbuk-uwem mbuk-uwem *(nom.1.10)* biography

mbuotidem *(nom.1)* faith

mbutidem *(nom.1)* trust

meenge *(act)* swallow

meitnerium *(sci)* meitnerium

melayu *(kw.1)* melayu

mem *(adj)* soft

mem *(adj)* weak

men *(nom.1)* swallow

mendelevium *(sci)* mendelevium

mercury *(sci)* mercury

metre *(nom.1)* metre

mfana *(nom.1)* trouble

mfana *(adj)* turbulent

mfana *(nom.1)* problem

mfana *(nom.1)* issue

mfang *(nom.1)* leaf

mfem *(nom.1)* cockroach

mfem *(nom.1)* beetle

mfet *(nom.1)* penis

mfin *(adv)* today

mfire *(nom.1)* brain

mfon *(adj)* gracious

mfon *(nom.1)* favour

mfon *(nom.1)* grace

mfri mfri *(nom.1.2)* cucumber

mfuk *(nom.1)* chin

mfuk *(nom.1)* cheek

mi *(adv)* here

mia *(nom.1)* beat

mia *(act)* clap

millet *(nom.1)* millet

million *(adj)* million

mint *(nom.1)* mint

miom *(act)* insult

miom *(nom.1)* insult

mkpa *(nom.1)* death

mkpa idem *(adj)* wonderful

mkpa-inuun *(nom.1)* ring

mkpafafagha *(nom.1)* armpit

mkpafang *(nom.1)* path

mkpafang *(nom.1)* gap

mkpan utong mkpan utong *(nom.1.2)* earring

mkpasi *(nom.1)* seed

mkpasip *(nom.1)* grain

mkpefiok *(nom.1)* regret

mkpekpem *(nom.1)* bat

mkpo *(pro)* it

mkpo *(act)* shout

mkpo *(adj)* loud

mkpo *(nom.1)* thing

mkpọ *(pro)* its

mkpo *(pro)* something

mkpo ekong *(nom.1)* weapon

mkpo imam *(adj)* amusing

mkpo isang *(nom.1)* caterpillar

mkpo isang *(act)* train

mkpo isang *(nom.1)* taxi

mkpo isang *(nom.1)* van

mkpo isang mkpo isang *(nom.1.2)* car

mkpo isang *(nom.1)* bus

mkpo isang *(nom.1)* motorcycle

mkpo isang *(nom.1)* vehicle

mkpo itie *(nom.1)* sofa

mkpo itong *(nom.2)* necklace

mkpo nna mkpo nna *(nom.1.2)*

bed

mkpo nsup *(adj)* mental

mkpo nyed usan *(nom.1)* sink

udori ibuot mkpo udod ibut *(nom.1.2)* pillow

mkpo udua *(nom.1)* product

mkpo ufuk iso mkpo ufuk iso *(nom.1.2)* mask

mkpo ukuhore efod mkpo ukuhore efod *(nom.1.2)* toilet roll

nkpo utuk edet mkpo usok inua *(nom.1.2)* toothbrush

mkpo usok inua *(nom.2)* toothpaste

mkpo utang-iko *(act)* phone

mkpo uting iko *(nom.2)* telephone

mkpo utom *(nom.1)* material

mkpo-awongho *(nom.1)* definition

mkpo-esed *(nom.1)* antiquity

mkpo-ibok *(nom.1)* fetish

mkpo-idoho *(nom.1)* nothing

mkpọ-isang *(nom.1)* scooter

mkpo-itie *(nom.1)* couch

mkpo-mbio *(nom.1)* trash

mkpo-nsop *(act)* possess

mkpo-ntipe *(nom.1)* consequence

mkpọ-ukpeme *(nom.1)* shield

mkpo-usin ebifik *(nom.1)* ventilator

mkpo-usio-ndise *(nom.1)* camera

mkpo-uting-iko *(nom.1)* microphone

mkpo-utom *(nom.1)* tool

mkpofioufiop *(nom.1)* butterfly

mkpoh *(nom.1)* catarrh

mkpok inua *(nom.1)* lip

mkpokobo *(nom.1)* prison

mkpon *(nom.1)* pride

mkpong *(adv)* yesterday

mkpọng *(act)* avoid

mkpong *(adv)* tomorrow

mkpọnọ *(nom.1)* chain

mkpri sokoro *(nom.1)* lime

mkum *(nom.1)* allergy

mma *(nom.1)* value

mmasang *(nom.1)* groundnut

mme adaha *(nom.1)* committee

mme mbet *(nom.1)* disciple

mme owo *(nom.1)* people

mme utor mme utor *(nom.1.2)* colour

mmeme *(act)* soften

mmeme *(adj)* easy

mmi *(nom.1)* here

mmi *(pos)* my

mmi *(pro)* myself

mmi doho *(cjn)* or

mmin *(nom.1)* liquor

mmin *(nom.1)* wine

mmin *(nom.1)* alcohol

mmiong *(act)* fart

mmo *(pro)* them

mmo *(pos)* their

mmong *(nom.1)* dew

mmong *(nom.2)* water

mmong *(nom.1)* liquid

mmong aben *(act)* drown

mmóng eba *(nom.1)* milk

mmong ikang *(nom.1)* kerosene

mmong itie kiet *(nom.1)* lake

mmor *(pre)* from

mmum ndian mmum ndiàn *(nom.1.2)* connection

Mohammed *(din.1)* Mohammed

molecule *(nom.1)* molecule

molybdenum *(sci)* molybdenum

mum *(act)* grab

mum *(act)* hold

muslim *(nom.1)* muslim

n *(ph)* n

nam *(nom.1)* process

nam *(act)* make

nam *(act)* claim

nam *(act)* construct

nam *(act)* treat

nam *(act)* do

nam nor *(nom.1)* doctor

nam-eyong *(act)* made up

nam-idiok *(act)* be evil

nam-ima *(act)* make love

Namibia *(nom.1)* Namibia

nanga-iba *(adj)* both

national *(adj)* national

nda eyo *(nom.1)* sunrise

nda-eyo *(nom.1)* summer

ndahare- nno *(nom.1)* forgiveness

ndang *(nom.1)* louse

nde *(adv)* too

ndedeng *(adj)* wet

ndedeng *(adj)* cold

ndedeng *(adj)* freezing

ndedibe *(nom.1)* secret

ndedibe *(adj)* secret

ndek *(adj)* raw

ndi ewod owo *(nom.1)* murder

ndi-yem *(nom.1)* demand

ndia uwem *(act)* enjoy

ndibene *(nom.2)* wall

ndidibe-mkpo *(nom.1)* mystery

ndien *(cjn)* and

ndien *(cjn)* then

ndien *(cjn)* nevertheless

ndien *(adv)* then

ndifop-mkpo *(act)* incinerate

ndik *(nom.10)* fear

ndik *(adj)* scary

ndikpe okuk *(nom.1)* deposit

ndikpe-okuk *(nom.1)* payment

ndikpọng-ndọ *(nom.1)* divorce

ndinoh *(nom.1)* delivery

ndiohoke *(adj)* unfamiliar

ndiọng *(nom.1)* flood

ndise ndise *(nom.1.2)* picture

ndise *(nom.1)* movie

ndise *(nom.1)* photograph

ndise *(nom.1)* passport

ndise *(act)* photograph

ndisi *(act)* row

ndisi *(adj)* alive

ndisiime *(nom.1)* nonsense

ndisime *(nom.1)* rubbish

ndisong-eyen *(nom.1)* scorn

ndisua *(nom.1)* contempt

ndito eka *(nom.2)* sibling

ndiyam *(nom.1)* trade

ndiyene-inem *(adj)* delightful

ndiyiip-owo *(adj)* little

ndiyiip-owo *(nom.1)* kidnapping

ndo *(act)* marry

ndo *(nom.2)* marriage

ndo *(act)* scare

ndó *(nom.1)* wedding

ndod-uyo *(act)* accuse

ndọk *(nom.1)* gossip

ndongesit *(act)* comfort

ndot uyo *(nom.1)* accusation

ndot uyo *(nom.1)* blame

nduba *(nom.1)* competition

ndubeghe *(act)* trade

ndubeghe *(nom.1)* business

ndubeghe *(nom.1)* trading

ndubeghe *(nom.1)* relationship

ndubire *(nom.1)* evening

ndudu *(nom.1)* hole

ndudue *(nom.1)* guilt

ndudwe *(nom.1)* mistake

nduk-odudu *(nom.1)* holiday

ndukóm-ekpe *(nom.1)* spider

ndung-ndiana *(nom.1)* neighbour

Nederlands *(nom.1)* Dutch

negative *(adj)* negative

nehe *(act)* arrange

nehe *(nom.1)* set

nem *(act)* trust

nem *(adj)* fun

neme *(act)* converse

neme *(act)* let ... know

nen *(act)* straighten

nen *(nom.1)* right

nen *(nom.1)* rights

neodymium *(sci)* neodymium

neon *(sci)* neon

neptunium *(sci)* neptunium

network *(nom.1)* network

neutron *(sci)* neutron

nfana nfana *(nom.1.10)* bully

nfere *(nom.1)* fruit

ngine *(nom.1)* machine

ngine *(nom.1)* engine

ngineer *(nom.1)* engineer

ngkanga *(adj)* empty

ngke *(nom.1)* parable

ngket *(act)* lead

ngket *(sci)* lead

ngkube *(nom.1)* athlete

ngkukumkpoyoriyo *(nom.1)* locust

ngwa ebek *(nom.1)* beard

ngwana *(act)* fight

ngwanga *(act)* clear

ngweem *(act)* lick

ngwene *(act)* flicker

ngwim *(act)* bear fruit

ngwo *(nom.1)* bribe

ngwo *(nom.1)* bribery

ngwo *(nom.1)* corruption

ngwong *(act)* drink

ngwong *(nom.1)* drink

ngwong kpa *(nom.1)* drunkard

nickel *(sci)* nickel

niin *(act)* doubt

niin *(act)* dispute

nim *(act)* maintain

nim *(act)* preserve

nim *(act)* believe

nim *(nom.1)* belief

nime *(act)* switch off

nime *(act)* turn off

niobium *(sci)* niobium

nitrogen *(sci)* nitrogen

nka *(nom.1)* age group

nka *(nom.1)* peer

nka *(act)* mate

nkang *(nom.1)* charcoal

nkanga *(adj)* mere

nkanika nkanika *(nom.1.2)* clock

nkanika *(nom.1)* bell

nkara *(adj)* cunning

nkara *(act)* trick

nkara *(act)* pretend

nkara *(nom.1)* hypocrisy

nke *(nom.1)* riddle

nké *(nom.1)* proverb

nkeng-idem *(adj)* gaudy

nkid-ikid *(nom.1)* owl

nkikid *(nom.1)* vision

nkikid *(act)* prophesy

nkokibout *(nom.1)* budget

nkon *(act)* snore

nkong ibok *(nom.1)* herb

nkop-item *(nom.1)* obedience

nkpo utem udia *(nom.1)* stove

nkwa *(nom.1)* bead

nkwa *(nom.1)* cube

nkwa eyen *(nom.1)* eyeball

nkwa-ibok *(nom.1)* tablet

nmo *(pro)* they

nmor *(adv)* where

nna-fon *(exc)* sleep tight

nne-nne *(adj)* correct

nne-nne *(adj)* upright

nneenem *(adj)* pleasant

nneme *(nom.1)* conversation

nneme *(nom.1)* communication

nnor *(act)* infect

nnuon ubok *(nom.1)* finger

nnuon ubok *(nom.1)* thumb

nnyin *(pro)* we

nnyin nnyin *(pos.1)* our

Noah *(nom.1)* Noah

nobelium *(sci)* nobelium

noono *(act)* give

nor *(act)* provide

north *(nom.1)* north

northern *(adj)* northern

Norway *(nom.1)* Norway

noun *(nom.1)* noun

nsa-isọng *(nom.1)* oware

nsad-isọng *(nom.1)* desert

nsaha-iso *(nom.1)* opposite

nsan nsan *(nom.1)* social distancing

nsek ayen akpo *(nom.2)* doll

nsek eyen nsek eyen *(nom.1.2)* baby

nsen unen *(nom.1)* egg

nsi-nsi *(adv)* forever

nsi-nsi *(adj)* everlasting

nsi-nsi *(nom.1)* infinity

nsido *(pro)* what

nsinsi *(adj)* eternal

nsinsi *(nom.1)* eternity

nsinsi *(adj)* permanent

nsio *(adj)* ostentatious

nsip- nsip *(adj)* slim

nsọngọ-mkpọ *(nom.1)* hardship

nsongurua *(adj)* expensive

nsu *(nom.1)* falsification

nsubó *(adv)* seldomly

nsuhuridem *(nom.1)* humility

nsungikang *(nom.1)* smoke

nta nta offiong *(nom.1)* star

ntaha *(adv)* why

ntak *(nom.1)* purpose

ntak *(nom.1)* reason

ntan *(nom.1)* sand

nte kiet *(adj)* any

ntie ntie efe *(nom.1.2)* place

ntiensé *(nom.1)* witness

nto *(nom.1)* environment

ntong *(nom.1)* dust

ntor ndaha *(nom.1)* station

ntoro *(exc)* yes

ntoro *(adj)* normal

ntre *(act)* be

ntuen ibok *(nom.1)* alligator pepper

ntukko *(nom.1)* fog

ntukon *(nom.1)* pepper

nua *(act)* push

nuakka *(act)* smash

nursery *(nom.1)* nursery

nwa ebek *(nom.1)* bear

nwa eyen *(nom.1)* eyelash

nwa eyen *(nom.1)* eyebrow

nwam *(act)* assist

nwam *(act)* support

nwana *(act)* strive

nwana *(act)* try

nwed *(nom.1)* writing

nwéd nwed *(nom.1.2)* book

nwed *(nom.1)* notebook

nwed ikó nwed iko *(nom.1.2)* dictionary

nwéd iko àbàsi nwed iko abasi *(nom.1.2)* bible

nwed usen-offiong *(nom.1)* calendar

nwed-akuk *(nom.1)* voucher

nwed-etop *(nom.1)* letter

nwed-etop *(nom.1)* newspaper

nwed-mbok *(nom.1)* magazine

nwed-okuk *(nom.1)* check

nwud *(act)* reveal

nya *(nom.1)* garden egg

nyahade mkpo *(adj)* lightweight

nyai *(act)* flatulate

nyam *(act)* sell

nyan *(adv)* forward

nyan *(nom.1)* point

nyek *(act)* tremble

nyek *(act)* shake

nyek *(act)* vibrate

nyeme *(act)* reject

nyen-edong *(nom.1)* lamb

nyianga *(act)* save

nyiik *(act)* whine

nyimme *(act)* squeeze

nyin *(pro)* ourselves

nyoo *(nom.1)* herring

nyọọ *(nom.1)* joke

nyoon *(act)* crawl

nyoong *(adj)* tall

nyoong *(adj)* long

o *(ph)* oa

obio *(nom.2)* country

obio *(nom.1)* Algeria

obio *(nom.1)* kingdom

obio *(nom.1)* nation

obio *(act)* state

obio *(nom.1)* town

obio *(nom.1)* state

obio *(nom.1)* state

obio *(nom.1)* city

obio *(nom.1)* Nigerian

obio idung *(nom.2)* Africa

obio idung obio idung *(nom.1.2)* Asia

obio idung obio idung *(nom.1.2)* Benin

obio idung *(nom.2)* Congo

obio idung *(nom.2)* Cote d'Ivoire

obio idung obio idung *(nom.1.2)* China

obio mbakara *(adj)* American

Obio Mbakara *(nom.1)* America

obio mbakara *(nom.1)* abroad

obio-mfia *(nom.1)* American

Obio-mfia Obio-Mfia *(nom.1.10)* London

Obio-Nyin *(nom.1)* Nigeria

objective *(nom.1)* objective

obod *(nom.1)* mountain

obong *(nom.1)* chief

ọbọng *(nom.1)* mosquito

Obong *(nom.1)* Lord

obong-osop *(exc)* godspeed

obongawan obongawan *(nom.1.2)* chairwoman

obongowo obongowo *(nom.1.2)* chairman

obongowo obongowo *(nom.1.2)* chairperson

obot-abasi *(nom.1)* temple

obuk *(nom.1)* flesh

odd *(adj)* odd

ódóró-itong *(nom.1)* avarice

odot *(act)* deserve

odot *(act)* be fitting

odudu *(nom.1)* permission

odudu *(nom.1)* energy

odudu *(nom.1)* power

odudu *(nom.1)* strength

odudu *(adj)* energetic

odudu *(sci)* charge

odudu *(adj)* powerful

oduma *(nom.1)* storm

offiong *(nom.1)* moon

offiong *(nom.1)* sun

offiong duop *(nom.1)* October

offiong duopeba *(nom.1)* December

offiong duopkiet *(nom.1)* November

Offiong Iba *(nom.1)* February

Offiong Inang *(nom.1)* April

offiong ita *(act)* march

Offiong Ita *(nom.1)* March

offiong itia-ita offiong itia-ita *(nom.1.2)* August

Offiong Itiaba *(nom.1)* July

offiong itiokeed *(nom.1)* June

Offiong Kiet *(nom.1)* January

offiong usukkiet offiong usukkiet *(nom.1.2)* September

ofon *(adj)* best

ọfọn *(adv)* well

ofong ofong *(nom.1.2)* clothes

ofong ofong *(nom.1.2)* dress

ofong *(nom.1)* attire

ọfọng *(nom.1)* fabric

ọfọng *(nom.1)* cloth

ofong idak idem *(nom.1)* underwear

ofong idem *(nom.1)* skirt

ofong inua ofong inua *(nom.1.2)* handkerchief

ofong ukwohore idem ofong ukohore idem *(nom.1.2)* towel

ofong ukot *(nom.1)* shorts

ofong ukot ofong ukot *(nom.1.2)* trouser

ofong usung ofong usung *(nom.1.2)* curtain

ofuri ofuri *(nom.1.2)* comprehension

oganesson *(nom.1)* Oganesson

okay *(exc)* okay

ókó-iyak *(nom.1)* fisherman

okoneyo *(nom.1)* night

okoti *(nom.1)* bean

okpo *(nom.1)* gallon

okpo *(nom.1)* skeleton

okpokoro okpokoro *(nom.1.2)* table

okposong *(adj)* chronic

okposong *(adj)* giant

ọkpọsọng *(nom.1)* difficulty

okposong *(adj)* great

okuk *(nom.1)* coin

okuk *(nom.1)* currency

okuk *(nom.1)* fees

okuk *(nom.1)* cash

okuk *(adj)* billion

okuk *(nom.2)* money

okuk mbet *(nom.1)* levy

okuk mbet *(nom.1)* tax

okuk udongo *(nom.1)* month

okuk-ndọ *(nom.1)* dowry

okuk-offiong *(nom.1)* salary

okuk-udongho *(nom.1)* therapist

ono-utom *(nom.1)* employee

ono-utom *(nom.1)* employer

oppose *(act)* oppose

organ *(nom.1)* organ

organizer *(nom.1)* organizer

osio mbere *(nom.1)* actor

Osita *(din)* Osita

osmium *(sci)* osmium

osong *(nom.1)* healing

osong *(adj)* tough

osong *(adj)* hard

osu-nsuk *(nom.1)* liar

otor iwang *(nom.1)* farmer

otu *(nom.1)* team

otu *(pre)* among

otu mme obio *(adj)* international

owo *(adj)* human

owo *(nom.1)* member

owo *(pro)* someone

owo *(nom.1)* human

owo *(nom.2)* person

owo ekong *(nom.1)* warrior

owo keere keed *(pro)* each and everyone

owo obio *(nom.1)* African

owo udongo *(adj)* disabled

owo-ekong *(nom.1)* soldier

owo-french *(nom.1)* French

owo-kiet *(nom.1)* one person

owo-udongho *(nom.1)* patient

oworo *(act)* mean

oworodidie *(nom.1)* meaning

owuo iso- owo *(adj)* famous

oxygen *(nom.1)* oxygen

oxygen *(sci)* oxygen

oyim *(nom.1)* onion

p *(ph)* p

paint *(nom.1)* paint

palladium *(sci)* palladium

parched *(adj)* parched

park *(nom.1)* park

parliamentarian *(nom.1)* parliamentarian

partner *(nom.1)* partner

party *(nom.1)* party

pedophile *(nom.1)* pedophile

penguin *(nom.1)* penguin

peppermint *(nom.1)* peppermint

perfume *(nom.1)* perfume

peter *(din.1)* Peter

petition *(nom.1)* petition

philosopher *(nom.1)* philosopher

phosphorus *(sci)* phosphorus

physics *(nom.1)* physics

piano *(nom.1)* piano

piggy-bank *(nom.1)* piggy bank

pijin *(kw.1)* Pidgin English

pinable *(nom.1)* pineapple

pink *(adj)* pink

pito *(nom.1)* pito

platinum *(sci)* platinum

pledge *(nom.1)* pledge

plutonium *(sci)* plutonium

pocket-money *(nom.1)* pocket money

poem *(nom.1)* poem

politicalparty *(nom.1)* political party

politician *(nom.1)* politician

polonium *(sci)* polonium

porcupine *(nom.1)* porcupine

possessive *(nom.1)* possessive

potassium *(sci)* potassium

powder-keg *(nom.1)* powder-keg

ppe *(nom.1)* personal protective equipment

praseodymium *(sci)* praseodymium

prawn *(nom.1)* prawn

prejudice *(nom.1)* prejudice

press *(nom.1)* press

print *(act)* print

printer *(nom.1)* printer

producer *(nom.1)* producer

promethium *(sci)* promethium

pronoun *(nom.1)* pronoun

prop *(act)* prop

protactinium *(sci)* protactinium

proton *(sci)* proton

punjabi *(nom.1)* Panjabi

puppet *(nom.1)* puppet

purple *(adj)* purple

puzzle *(nom.1)* puzzle

q *(ph)* q

quotation *(nom.1)* quotation

r *(ph)* r

radiation *(sci)* radiation

radium *(sci)* radium

radon *(sci)* radon

rainbow *(nom.1)* rainbow

raisin *(nom.1)* raisin

rand *(nom.1)* rand

razor *(nom.1)* razor

rebel *(nom.1)* rebel

rebellion *(nom.1)* rebellion

record *(act)* record

rectangle *(nom.1)* rectangle

reliable *(adj)* reliable

remote-control *(nom.1)* remote control

return *(act)* return

rhenium *(sci)* rhenium

rhodium *(sci)* rhodium

risk *(nom.1)* risk

rocket *(nom.1)* rocket

roentgenium *(sci)* roentgenium

Romans *(nom.1)* Romans

rubidium *(sci)* rubidium

Ruski *(kw.1)* ruski

ruthenium *(sci)* ruthenium

rutherfordium *(sci)* rutherfordium

s *(ph)* s

saak *(act)* laugh

saap *(act)* poke

saat *(act)* dry

saat *(adj)* dry

sakka *(act)* explode

samarium *(sci)* samarium

sana *(nom.1)* cleanliness

sana *(adj)* clean

sang *(act)* move

sanga *(act)* stroll

sanitizer *(nom.1)* sanitizer

sappa *(adj)* active

sarcasm *(nom.1)* sarcasm

sat *(act)* select

sauce *(nom.1)* sauce

scandium *(sci)* scandium

science *(nom.1)* science

se *(act)* look

se *(nom.1)* spy

se *(act)* spy

se *(act)* see

seaborgium *(sci)* seaborgium

secondary school *(nom.1)* high-school

sed *(nom.1)* resurrection

selenium *(sci)* selenium

seme *(act)* grieve

seme *(nom.1)* sorrow

sequence *(nom.1)* sequence

sex-education *(nom.1)* sex education

sh *(ph)* sh

shape *(nom.1)* structure

sheabutter *(nom.1)* sheabutter

Shona *(nom.1)* Shona

ufok-nwed *(nom.1)* school

si-isine *(act)* consist

si-isine *(nom.1)* content

sia *(cjn)* because

siaak *(act)* mention

siaak *(act)* split

siaak *(act)* divide

siaak *(nom.1)* explanation

sian *(act)* announce

siere *(nom.1)* dawn

sign *(nom.1)* sign

siime *(adj)* foolish

siit *(act)* block

sik *(act)* adjust

sik-da *(exc)* excuse me

sika *(nom.1)* cigarette

silicon *(sci)* silicon

silver *(nom.1)* silver

silver *(sci)* silver

sim *(act)* reach

sim-à-akpatere-ntor *(act)* reach a final milestone

sin *(act)* fill

sin *(act)* score

sin *(act)* put

sin *(act)* replace

sin *(nom.1)* inclusion

sin-ebeeñe *(nom.1)* application

sine *(act)* wear

sio *(act)* deduct

sio *(act)* withdraw

sio *(act)* discard

sio *(act)* drain

sio *(act)* nominate

sio *(act)* remove

sio *(act)* subtract

sio *(act)* reduce

sio ke utom *(nom.1)* sack

sio-nyam *(act)* retail

sioop *(act)* sigh

smoking-pipe *(nom.1)* pipe

sodium *(sci)* sodium

sok *(act)* scrub

sokoro *(nom.1)* orange

sokoro *(adj)* orange

somewhere *(pro)* somewhere

song *(nom.1)* vitality

song *(adj)* strong

song-odudu *(adj)* serious

soop *(adj)* quick

sop *(act)* disappear

sop *(act)* hurry

sop *(adv)* quickly

sosongo *(nom.1)* thanks

sosongoh *(exc)* thanks

Sotho *(nom.1)* Sotho

source *(nom.1)* source

south *(nom.1)* south

South-Sudan *(nom.1)* South Sudan

southern *(adj)* southern

soyo *(act)* descend

spinning top *(nom.1)* spinning top

sport *(nom.1)* sport

spring *(nom.1)* spring

steer *(act)* steer

step *(act)* step

stop *(nom.1)* information

stripe *(nom.1)* stripe

strontium *(sci)* strontium

sua *(act)* hate

sua *(nom.1)* hatred

suaan *(act)* scatter

suagha *(adj)* dishevelled

suene *(act)* disgrace

suene *(nom.1)* humiliation

sugho *(act)* lie

suk *(act)* see ... off

suka *(nom.1)* sugar

sukho idem *(act)* soothe

sulfur *(sci)* sulfur

summarization *(nom.1)* summarisation

sung *(nom.1)* safety

sung *(adj)* gentle

sung *(adj)* safe

sung *(nom.1)* soothing

sung-sung *(adv)* slowly

sung-sung *(adj)* slow

suob suop *(nom.1.2)* soap

Suomi *(nom.1)* Finnish

suóp *(adj)* fast

suóp *(act)* fast

suop *(nom.1)* rap

suóp *(nom.1)* speed

sushi *(nom.1)* sushi

suugho *(adj)* humble

suugho *(adj)* comfortable

swan *(act)* spread

Swati *(nom.1)* Swati

sweng *(act)* abuse

t *(ph)* t

ta *(act)* chew

ta-mkpo *(act)* masticate

taagha *(act)* tattered

tad *(act)* loosen

Takoradi *(nom.1)* Takoradi

tama *(act)* jump

tang *(act)* speak

tang *(act)* braid

tantalum *(sci)* tantalum

tebe *(act)* stink

tebe *(act)* smile

technetium *(sci)* technetium

technology *(nom.1)* technology

tee *(act)* remember

teghe *(act)* decrease

tehe *(act)* calm

telescope *(nom.1)* telescope

tellurium *(sci)* tellurium

tem *(act)* cook

tém *(act)* boil

temme *(act)* explain

terbium *(sci)* terbium

thallium *(sci)* thallium

therefore *(adv)* therefore

thorium *(sci)* thorium

threat *(nom.1)* threat

thulium *(sci)* thulium

thunderbolt *(nom.1)* thunderbolt

ti *(nom.1)* tea

tiaara *(adv)* often

tibe *(act)* happen

tibe *(act)* sprout

tie *(act)* sit

tiip *(act)* carve

tim *(nom.1)* bullying

tim *(act)* pound

tim *(act)* beat

timede *(nom.1)* confusion

timere *(adj)* chaotic

ting *(nom.1)* discussion

ting *(act)* talk

titanium *(sci)* titanium

tithe *(nom.1)* tithe

tiyo *(nom.1)* memorization

tó *(act)* drop

toffee *(nom.1)* toffee

toh *(act)* sow

toh *(nom.1)* plant

toh *(act)* plant

toi *(act)* wake

tọi *(act)* awaken

tok – tumbuka

tok *(act)* urinate

tok *(act)* thicken

tom *(nom.1)* kiss

tomato *(nom.1)* tomato

tọmtọm *(nom.1)* pigeon

tongho *(act)* begin

tongho *(nom.1)* beginner

tongo *(adj)* cloudy

top *(act)* throw

top *(act)* shoot

top-duook *(act)* throw away

toro *(act)* defecate

toro *(act)* commend

tosin *(adj)* thousands

tot *(act)* increase

tour *(nom.1)* tour

toyo *(act)* remind

traffic *(nom.1)* traffic

train *(nom.1)* train

transportation *(nom.1)* transportation

trillion *(adj)* trillion

truck *(nom.1)* truck

tua *(act)* cry

tuagha *(act)* bump into

tuagha *(pro)* having

tuho *(act)* start

tuko *(act)* torment

tuko *(act)* manage

tuko *(act)* punish

tum *(act)* peck

tum *(act)* kiss

tumbuka *(nom.1)* Tumbuka

tungsten *(sci)* tungsten

turkey *(nom.1)* turkey

tutu *(adv)* very

tuuk *(act)* touch

tweet *(act)* tweet

twelfth *(adj)* twelfth

u *(ph)* u

ubaak *(det)* some

ubaha-usen *(nom.1)* morning

ubak *(nom.1)* half

ubak-ini *(adv)* sometimes

ubanga *(nom.1)* diversity

ubed ubed *(nom.1.2)* room

ubehe ubehe *(nom.1.2)* concern

ubiad-okuk *(nom.1)* expense

ubiak *(nom.1)* pain

ubiak ibuot *(nom.1)* headache

ubiak-idib *(nom.1)* stomach-ache

ubiak-usen *(nom.1)* wee hours

ubiong utom *(adj)* responsible

ubod mkpo *(adj)* creative

uboho *(nom.1)* freedom

uboho *(adj)* free

ubok *(nom.1)* arm

ubok *(nom.1)* hand

ubók utom *(nom.1)* responsibility

ubók-akuk *(nom.1)* saving

ubom *(nom.1)* boat

ubom mmong *(nom.1)* canoe

ubom nsungikang *(nom.1)* ship

ubom onyong ubom onyong *(nom.1.2)* aeroplane

ubom onyong *(nom.1)* helicopter

ubom-eyong *(nom.1)* plane

udebe *(adj)* soaked

udebep *(nom.1)* shopping

udi *(nom.1)* grave

udia udia *(nom.1.2)* food

udia mbebri-eyo *(act)* dine

udia usiere udia usiere *(nom.1.2)* breakfast

udiana unwam *(nom.1.2)* assistant

udip *(nom.1)* mushroom

udit *(act)* force

udit *(nom.1)* force

udo-obod *(nom.1)* police

udob *(adj)* heavy

udod *(nom.1)* interest

udod ayeyen udod ayeyen *(nom.1.2)* greatgrandchild

udok usung *(nom.1.2)* door

udók *(nom.1)* spade

udok mmong *(nom.1)* baptism

udom *(adj)* right

udomo *(nom.1)* test

udomo *(nom.1)* exam

udong *(adj)* desirable

udong *(act)* stimulate

udong *(nom.1)* thirst

udong *(nom.1)* need

udong *(act)* need

udong *(nom.1)* wish

udong *(nom.1)* passion

udong-ekikoi *(nom.1)* nausea

udongho *(nom.1)* seizure

udongho *(nom.1)* illness

udongo *(nom.1)* sickness

udongo *(nom.1)* disease

udongo udongo *(nom.1.2)* virus

udongo *(adj)* sick

udongo utoro *(nom.1)* diarrhoea

udop *(nom.1)* weight

udot-inua *(nom.1)* lipbalm

udua *(nom.1)* market

udua *(nom.1)* week

udua *(nom.1)* commerce

udua ufok *(nom.1)* storehouse

udua ufok udua ufok *(nom.1.2)* store

udua-mkpo *(nom.1)* price

udud *(act)* strengthen

uduk *(nom.1)* rope

uduk *(act)* gain

uduk *(nom.1)* profit

uduk *(nom.1)* income

uduk akpó *(adj)* elastic

uduk-ikot *(nom.1)* snake

ufa *(adj)* new

ufa-aboikpa *(adj)* teenage

ufad-mkpo *(nom.1)* scissors

ufan *(nom.1)* friendship

ufan ufan *(nom.1.2)* friend

ufan owowan ufan awo-nwan *(nom.1.2)* girlfriend

ufan awoden *(nom.2)* boyfriend

ufang *(sci)* space

ufang *(act)* free

ufang *(adj)* wide

ufang *(nom.1)* verse

ufen *(nom.1)* suffering

ufen *(act)* suffer

ufen *(nom.1)* stress

ufene *(nom.1)* pet

ufia *(act)* slap

ufia *(act)* spank

ufiin *(adj)* left

ufik *(act)* smell

ufịk *(adj)* fragrant

ufịk *(nom.1)* fragrance

ufik *(nom.1)* smell

ufik-ubok *(act)* vote

ufiop *(nom.1)* heat

ufiop *(act)* heat

ufiop *(adj)* hot

ufiop idem *(nom.1)* fever

ufiop ofong ufiop ofong *(nom.1.2)* blanket

ufod *(nom.1)* centre

ufok *(nom.1)* building

ufok ufok *(nom.1.2)* home

ufok ufok *(nom.1.2)* house

ufok emana ufok *(nom.1.2)* family

ufok abasi *(nom.1)* church

ufok ibok *(nom.1)* hospital

ufok ibok *(nom.1)* clinic

ufok inuen *(act)* roost

ufok mkpakop *(nom.1)* cell

ufok mkpo *(nom.1)* tent

ufok nde idap ufok nde idap *(nom.1.2)* bedroom

ufok nwed ntok eyen *(nom.1)* primary school

ufok ubon-mkpo *(nom.1)* warehouse

ufok urua ufok udua *(nom.1.2)*

shop

ufok uka ifuo *(nom.2)* toilet

ufok ukpep mkpo *(nom.1)* class-room

ufok utom *(nom.1)* office

ufok uyere idem ufok uyere idem *(nom.1.2)* shower

ufok-isong *(nom.1)* bungalow

ufok-mbed *(nom.1)* parliament

ufok-motor *(nom.1)* garage

ufok-nwed *(nom.1)* college

ufok-nwed *(nom.1)* education

ufok-obong *(nom.1)* palace

ufon *(nom.1)* advantage

uforo *(nom.1)* success

uforo *(nom.1)* progress

uforo *(adj)* fertile

ufot-eyong *(nom.1)* hemisphere

ufrafirai-iyak *(nom.1)* fried-fish

ufuk-eyo *(nom.1)* umbrella

ufuot *(nom.1)* middle

ugwed-anying *(nom.1)* registration

ukara *(nom.1)* rule

ukara *(nom.1)* governance

ukelele *(nom.1)* ukelele

ukem *(adj)* equal

ukem *(adj)* same

ukeme *(nom.1)* courage

ukeme *(nom.1)* effort

ukeme *(adj)* capable

ukeme *(adj)* able

ukeme *(nom.1)* competence

ukut iso ukid iso *(nom.1.2)* mirror

uko *(adj)* brave

uko *(adj)* bold

uko *(adj)* arrogant

uko *(adj)* courageous

uko *(act)* command

uko *(nom.1)* command

uko uko *(nom.1.2)* arrogance

uko *(nom.1)* liability

ukod ukod *(nom.1.2)* beer

ukom *(nom.1)* plantain

ukọp *(nom.1)* cover

ukot *(nom.1)* leg

ukot *(nom.1)* toe

ukot *(nom.1)* inlaw

ukot-nsung *(nom.1)* palmwine

ukpa *(nom.1)* quantity

ukpeme *(act)* guard

ukpeme *(nom.1)* protection

ukpeme-ekọng *(nom.1)* rear-guard

ukpep *(nom.1)* learning

ukpep mkpo *(nom.1)* lesson

ukpohore *(nom.2)* key

ukpong *(nom.1)* spirit

ukpong *(nom.1)* soul

ukpono *(act)* dignify

ukpuhore *(act)* change

ukuk udongoh *(nom.1)* nurse

ukung *(act)* fuck

ukup *(nom.1)* lid

ukwak *(nom.1)* metal

ukwak *(nom.1)* nail

ukwak *(sci)* iron

ukwo-edim *(nom.1)* rainy season

ukwok ukod ukwok ukod *(nom.1.2)* carpet

uma *(nom.1)* miser

uma *(nom.1)* mister

uma *(adj)* miserly

uman-edọng *(nom.1)* ewe

umiang *(adj)* several

umiang *(adv)* very much

umiang-owo *(nom.1)* crowd

umono-eyen *(nom.1)* lens

una *(nom.1)* scarcity

una utom *(adj)* unemployed

una-ukpono *(act)* dishonor

unadot *(nom.1)* universe

unam *(nom.1)* pork

unam *(nom.1)* beef

unam *(nom.1)* meat

unam unam *(nom.1.2)* animal

unan *(act)* injure

undesirable *(adj)* undesirable

Uneghe *(nom.1)* Igbo

unek *(act)* dance

unek *(nom.1)* ballet

unen unen *(nom.1.2)* chicken

unen *(nom.1)* liberty

unen *(nom.1)* hen

unen *(nom.1)* fowl

unen abeke *(nom.1)* duck

unen abeke *(nom.1)* guinea-fowl

ungrateful *(adj)* ungrateful

unie *(nom.1)* owner

unie-eyen *(nom.1)* parents

unie-obio *(nom.1)* citizen

unie-ufok *(nom.1)* landlord

unnuen *(nom.1)* syringe

unor ibok *(act)* vaccinate

unuen-ye-unuen *(nom.1)* pins and needles

ununtrium *(sci)* ununtrium

wam unwam *(nom.1.2)* help

unwam *(act)* help

urak-ayaebot *(nom.1)* grape

uranium *(sci)* uranium

USA *(nom.1)* USA

usan udia usan *(nom.1.2)* plate

useme *(nom.1)* fool

useme *(nom.1)* dimwit

usen *(nom.1)* day

usen *(adv)* daily

usen inang ke udua *(nom.1)* Thursday

usen-emana *(nom.1)* birthday

usen-ọfiọng *(nom.1)* date

usiere *(nom.1)* daybreak

usin usin *(nom.1.2)* bonus

usin-eyen *(nom.1)* envy

usio-mbire *(adj)* entertaining

uso *(nom.1)* skill

usok-mkpo *(nom.1)* eraser

usong *(nom.1)* street

usong-eyen *(nom.1)* insults

usoro *(nom.1)* festival

usoro-mkpa *(nom.1)* funeral

usua *(nom.1)* enemy

usuk-usuk *(adj)* careful

usuk-usuk *(nom.1)* carefulness

usukkiet *(adj)* nine

usuku ibuot *(adj)* loyal

usung *(nom.1)* road

usung *(nom.1)* highway

usung *(nom.1)* fufu

usung *(nom.1)* way

usung afum *(nom.1)* window

usung isang usung isang *(nom.1.2)* journey

usung-edinam *(nom.1)* technique

usung-eyen *(act)* dishonour

utede *(nom.1)* vulture

utid-udia *(nom.1)* fasting

utin *(adj)* sunny

uto *(nom.1)* story

uto-eyen *(nom.1)* malaria

utom *(nom.1)* duty

utom *(nom.1)* job

utom *(act)* work

utom utom *(nom.1.2)* work

utom eto utom eto *(nom.1.2)* carpentry

utong *(nom.1)* ear

utor *(nom.1)* type

utor *(act)* type

utor-nte-ayem *(exc)* such as this

utuk *(act)* cheat

utum-kama *(act)* value

utung *(nom.1)* worm

uwa *(nom.1)* destiny

uwak *(adj)* bountiful

uwak *(adj)* abundant

uwak *(nom.1)* lot

uwak *(adv)* more

uwak *(adv)* too much

uwak *(adj)* plentiful

uwak *(adj)* how much

uwak *(adj)* many

uwana *(nom.1)* light

uwana *(adj)* bright

uween *(nom.1)* needle

uweene *(nom.1)* poverty

uweene *(nom.1)* pauper

uwem *(nom.1)* life

uweme-eyo *(nom.1)* afternoon

uwene *(nom.1)* indigent

uwoho-iyiip *(act)* bleed

uwoho-iyiip *(nom.1)* bleeding

uwud mkpó *(nom.1)* campaign

uwud-mkpo uwud mkpo *(nom.1.2)* example

uwud-mkpo *(nom.1)* representative

uyagha *(adj)* wasted

uyaha *(act)* deplete

uyai *(nom.1)* beauty

uyai *(adj)* pretty

uyai mfang *(nom.1)* flower

uyai mkpo *(nom.1)* aesthetic

uyai-mkpo *(nom.1)* gold

uyim *(nom.1)* selfishness

uyim *(nom.1)* stinginess

uyime *(act)* approve

uyime *(nom.1)* decision

uyime *(nom.1)* agreement

uyio *(act)* order

uyo *(nom.1)* bread

uyo *(nom.1)* voice

uyo *(nom.1)* order

uyom *(nom.1)* sound

uyom *(nom.1)* noise

v *(ph)* v

valiant *(adj)* valiant

vanadium *(sci)* vanadium

venda *(nom.1)* Venda

venom *(nom.1)* venom

verb *(nom.1)* verb

video *(nom.1)* video

vim *(nom.1)* vim

violet *(adj)* violet

vowel *(nom.1)* vowel

w *(ph)* w

wa *(nom.1)* sacrifice

waah *(exc)* waah

waak *(act)* mix

waak *(act)* tear

waak *(nom.1)* tear

wad *(act)* drive

wana ndi ting *(act)* insinuate

wara *(act)* say goodbye

watermelon *(nom.1)* watermelon

waya *(act)* sneeze

web *(nom.1)* web

website *(nom.1)* website

weene *(adj)* poor

wek *(act)* breathe

west *(nom.1)* west

wet *(act)* write

wield *(act)* wield

will *(nom.1)* will

wọfa *(nom.1)* guava

wogho *(act)* swear

wok *(act)* swim

wolaytta *(kw.1)* wolaytta

wond *(nom.1)* miss

woro *(act)* deflate

woro *(act)* exit

woro *(act)* log out

woro *(act)* flow

wot *(act)* kill

wuot *(act)* lend

wut *(act)* show

wut *(act)* desire

x *(ph)* x

xenon *(sci)* xenon

xylopia *(nom.1)* xylopia

y *(ph)* y

yaat *(nom.1)* yard

yaha *(adv)* as

yaha *(act)* rescue

yak *(act)* let

yak *(act)* allow

yak amana *(adv)* later

yama *(adj)* glossy

yama *(act)* shine

yaresit *(act)* annoy

yaws *(nom.1)* yaws

ye *(cjn)* with

ye *(pro)* ye

ye *(adv)* and

yeh *(act)* shower

yene *(act)* get

yene *(act)* have

yene *(act)* recover

yene-a-mum-ke *(act)* have a hold on

yenesis *(nom.1)* Genesis

yet *(act)* wash

yet *(act)* melt

yib *(act)* steal

yiip *(act)* pinch

yime *(act)* admit

yiré *(exc)* emphasis

yire *(act)* pursue

yire *(act)* persecute

yit *(act)* attach

yo *(nom.1)* tolerance

Yohn *(din.1)* John

yommo *(adj)* pregnant

yong *(act)* roam

youe *(pro)* you

youes *(pro)* you

yous *(pro)* you

ytterbium *(sci)* ytterbium

yttrium *(sci)* yttrium

yuhu *(act)* surround

yum *(act)* want

yum *(act)* search

yum *(act)* seek

yum *(act)* find

yumo *(act)* say

z *(ph)* z

Zambia *(nom.1)* Zambia

zambian *(adj)* Zambian

zebra *(nom.1)* zebra

Zimbabwe *(nom.1)* Zimbabwe

Zimbabwean *(nom.1)* Zimbabwean

zinc *(sci)* zinc

zirconium *(sci)* zirconium

zoology *(sci)* zoology

zulu *(nom.1)* Zulu

Index

24 *24*, 38
365 *365*, 39
366 *366*, 39

a *a*, 13, 16, 38, 48, 55, 58
a little *ekpri*, 79
abdomen *edak edak*, 76
able *ukeme*, 133
abomination *idiok-mkpo*, 88
about *abagha*, 58
above *abogho*, 58
abroad *obio mbakara*, 116
abundant *uwak*, 137
abuse *sweng*, 126
accept *bo*, 69
acceptance *bo*, 69
accident *accident*, 58
account *ibad*, 86
accountability *ibad*, 86
accounting *ibad ibad*, 86
accounts *ibad*, 86
accusation *ndot uyo*, 109
accuse *ndod-uyo*, 109
achieve *ino mkpo inam*, 92
acidic *acidic*, 58

act *edinam*, 76
action *edinàm*, 15, 76
active *sappa*, 122
activity *edinam*, 76
actor *osio mbere*, 118
actress *asio-mbere*, 64
actual *ata*, 65
add *dian*, 72
address *address*, 59
ademe *ademe*, 59
adequate *afon-akem*, 60
adjective *adjective*, 59
adjust *sik*, 123
administration *ada-ibout*, 58
admire *ma*, 101
admit *yime*, 141
adoption *adoption*, 59
adore *ma*, 101
adult *akaba owo*, 60
adultery *ina-esin*, 91
advance *iso*, 93
advantage *ufon*, 133
adverb *adverb*, 59
advertisement *advertisement*, 59

advice *item*, 93
aeroplane *ubom onyong ubom ony-
    ong*, 129
aeroplane *ubom onyong*, 41
aesthetic *uyai mkpo*, 138
affair *affair*, 59
affection *ima*, 90
Afghanistan *Afghanistan*, 59
Africa *obio idung*, 115
African *african*, 60
African *owo obio*, 119
afternoon *uweme-eyo*, 39, 138
again *fiak*, 83
age *isua*, 93
age group *nka*, 111
agreement *uyime*, 138
air *afim*, 59
airconditioner *akeme afum akeme
    afum*, 61
Ajoa *Ajoa*, 60
Akan *akan*, 60
alcohol *mmin*, 106
algebra *algebra*, 63
Algeria *obio*, 115
algorithm *algorithm*, 63
alive *ndisi*, 108
all *afed*, 59
all *afit*, 60
allergic *akum*, 62
allergy *mkum*, 106
alligator *afiom*, 60
alligator pepper *ntuen ibok*, 113
allow *yak*, 140

Almighty *akwa*, 62
almighty *akwa*, 62
alone *ikpong*, 90
aluminum *aluminum*, 63
always *afed-ini*, 59
Ama *Ama*, 63
amen *amen*, 63
America *Obio Mbakara*, 115
American *obio mbakara*, 115
American *obio-mfia*, 116
americium *americium*, 63
among *otu*, 119
amount *ibad*, 86
amusing *mkpo imam*, 104
ancestor *mme usor usor ette ette*,
    82
ancient *eset*, 80
ancient times *eset*, 80
and *ndien*, 108
and *ye*, 140
angel *angel*, 63
anger *iyaresit*, 95
animal *unam unam*, 135
animal *unam*, 35
anise *anise anise*, 64
aniseed *aniseed*, 64
ankle *itong ukot*, 94
announce *sian*, 123
annoy *yaresit*, 140
annoying *iyaresit*, 95
another *efen*, 77
answer *iboro iboro*, 86
answer *iboro*, 86

INDEX – INDEX

ant *akpa-isong*, 61
antelope *antelope*, 64
antimony *antimony*, 64
antiquity *mkpo-esed*, 105
anvil *anvil*, 64
any *nte kiet*, 113
apple *apple*, 64
application *sin-ebeeñe*, 124
appreciate *ekom*, 78
apprentice *akpep-utom*, 62
approach *kpere*, 99
approve *uyime*, 138
April *Offiong Inang*, 117
Arabic *Arabiya*, 64
argon *argon*, 64
argue *faanga*, 83
argument *faanga*, 82
arithmetic *arithmetic*, 64
arm *ubok*, 129
armpit *mkpafafagha*, 104
arrange *nehe*, 109
arrogance *uko uko*, 134
arrogant *uko*, 134
arrow *idang idang*, 87
arsenic *arsenic*, 64
art *art*, 64
artery *asip asip*, 65
artist *osio mbere asip*, 65
as *yaha*, 140
Asia *obio idung obio idung*, 115
ask *bep*, 15, 68
aspiration *idorenyin*, 88
asset *iyene*, 95

assist *nwam*, 114
assistant *udiana unwam*, 130
association *mboho*, 102
astatine *astatine*, 65
at *ke*, 15, 96
athlete *ngkube*, 110
Atlantic *atlantic*, 65
atom *atom*, 65
attach *yit*, 141
attire *ofong*, 117
August *offiong itia-ita offiong itia-ita*, 117
August *offiong itia-ita*, 40
aunt *awowan eyeneka ete(eka)*, 42, 66
auntie *ayeneka ete ayeneka ete,eka awowan*, 66
Australia *australia*, 65
authority *akpotiod akpotiod*, 62
Autumn *autumn*, 65
avarice *ódóró-itong*, 116
avoid *mkpọng*, 106
awaken *tọi*, 127
award *eno*, 80
awesome *awesome*, 66
ay *e*, 75
aye *aye*, 66
ayoyo *ayoyo*, 67
azonto *azonto*, 67

b *b*, 67
baby *nsek eyen nsek eyen*, 112
back *edem*, 76
back of the head *edem-ibuot*, 76

backlog *backlog*, 67
backspace *ka edem*, 96
backyard *edem-esa*, 76
bad *diok*, 73
bag *ekpat*, 78
ball *mbri ikpa mbra ikpa*, 102
ballet *unek*, 135
balloon *bolom-bolom*, 69
Bambara *bambara*, 67
banana *mboro*, 102
bank *itie usin okuk*, 94
banker *banker*, 67
baptism *udok mmong*, 130
barium *barium*, 67
bark *kpoi*, 99
barrel *barrel*, 67
basin *besin*, 68
basket *akpasa*, 62
basketball *basketball*, 67
bat *mkpekpem*, 104
battle *ekong*, 78
be *ntre*, 19, 42, 48, 55, 113
be big *ado-ekamba*, 59
be drunk *awung-kpa*, 66
be evil *nam-idiok*, 107
be fitting *odot*, 116
be good *ba-afon*, 67
be last *do-akpatere*, 73
be lengthy *aniong*, 64
be shy *kop-buut*, 98
beach *beach*, 67
bead *nkwa*, 112
beaker *beaker*, 68

bean *okoti*, 118
bear *nwa ebek*, 114
bear fruit *ngwim*, 110
beard *ngwa ebek*, 110
beat *ibit-ikwo*, 86
beat *mia*, 103
beat *tim*, 127
beautiful *ayaiya*, 66
beauty *uyai*, 138
because *sia*, 123
become *do*, 73
bed *mkpo nna mkpo nna*, 105
bedroom *ufok nde idap ufok nde idap*, 132
bedstead *eto-bed*, 81
bee *akuọk*, 62
beef *unam*, 135
beer *ukod ukod*, 134
beetle *mfem*, 103
befit *dot*, 74
before *mbem-iso*, 15, 102
beg *beenge*, 68
begin *tongho*, 128
beginner *tongho*, 128
beginning *editongo editongo*, 77
behaviour *ido ido*, 88
being *awo*, 66
belch *bekke*, 68
belief *nim*, 111
believe *nim*, 111
bell *nkanika*, 111
beloved *edima*, 76
belt *ikpa-isin*, 90

Bemba *bemba*, 68
bench *akpakara*, 61
Benin *obio idung obio idung*, 115
berkelium *berkelium*, 68
beryllium *beryllium*, 68
best *ofon*, 117
betray *bia*, 68
better *afon*, 60
bible *nwéd iko àbàsi nwed iko abasi* 114
bicycle *enang ukwak*, 41, 80
big *akamba*, 60
bile *bile*, 69
bill *bill*, 69
billion *okuk*, 118
biography *mbuk-uwem mbuk-uwem* 102
bird *inuen inuen*, 92
birth *emana*, 79
birth *man*, 79
birthday *usen-emana*, 136
bismuth *bismuth*, 69
black *abubit*, 14, 41, 58
blacksmith *blacksmith*, 69
blame *ndot uyo*, 109
blanket *ufiop ofong ufiop ofong*, 132
blazing *fop*, 83
bleed *uwoho-iyiip*, 138
bleeding *uwoho-iyiip*, 138
blessing *edidiọng*, 76
block *siit*, 123
blog *blog*, 69

blood *iyiip*, 95
blow *fit*, 83
blow *ita*, 93
blue *blue*, 41, 69
boat *ubom*, 129
bodice *itóng-ofong*, 94
body *idem idem*, 87
bohrium *bohrium*, 69
,boil *tém*, 127
bold *uko*, 134
bomb *bomb*, 69
bone *akpo*, 62
bonus *usin usin*, 136
book *danga*, 72
book *nwéd nwed*, 114
bọok *nwéd*, 55
boring *idob*, 88
boron *boron*, 70
boss *ete/eka ufok*, 81
both *nanga-iba*, 107
bother *fino*, 83
bottle *ekpeme*, 79
boundary *adanga*, 58
bountiful *uwak*, 137
bow *idang*, 87
box *ekeme*, 78
boy *akparawa eden*, 62
boy *akparawa*, 12, 16, 35
boyfriend *ufan awoden*, 131
bracket *bracket*, 70
braid *tang*, 126
brain *mfire*, 103
brave *uko*, 134

bread *uyo*, 138
breadth *ibifik ibifik*, 86
break *bom*, 69
breakfast *udia usiere udia usiere*, 130
breast *eba*, 75
breathe *wek*, 139
bribe *ngwo*, 110
bribery *ngwo*, 110
bridge *ebup*, 75
brief *imuk*, 91
bright *uwana*, 138
bring *ben-di*, 68
broad *kpon*, 99
bromine *bromine*, 70
brother *eyeneka owoden ayeneka awoden*, 66
brown *brown*, 70
bruise *mbon unan*, 102
bucket *akpo-mmong*, 62
budget *nkokibout*, 111
buffer *buffer*, 70
build *limal*, 100
building *ufok*, 132
bully *fiomo*, 83
bully *nfana nfana*, 110
bullying *tim*, 127
bump into *tuagha*, 128
bungalow *ufok-isong*, 133
burn *fop*, 83
bus *mkpo isang*, 104
business *ndubeghe*, 109
busy *dukpo*, 74

butter *butter*, 70
butterfly *mkpofioufiop*, 105
button *button*, 70
buy *deb*, 72
buyer *andidep*, 63
by *by*, 70
bye *ka-di*, 96

cabbage *cabbage*, 70
cadmium *cadmium*, 70
caesium *caesium*, 70
cake *cake*, 70
calabash *iko*, 89
calcium *calcium*, 70
calculus *calculus*, 70
calendar *nwed usen-offiong*, 114
californium *californium*, 70
call *kud*, 100
calm *tehe*, 126
camel *eniang mbiomo*, 80
camera *mkpo-usio-ndise*, 105
Cameroon *Cameroon*, 70
camp *camp*, 70
campaign *uwud mkpó*, 138
Canada *canada*, 70
cane *ikpa*, 90
canoe *ubom mmong*, 129
capable *ukeme*, 133
capital *capital*, 70
car *mkpo isang mkpo isang*, 104
car *mkpo isang*, 41
carbon *carbon*, 70
card *card*, 70
care *kom*, 98

careful *usuk-usuk*, 136
carefulness *usuk-usuk*, 136
caress *forho*, 84
carpenter *akong eto akong eto*, 61
carpentry *utom eto utom eto*, 137
carpet *ukwok ukod ukwok ukod*, 135
carrot *carrot*, 70
cartoon *cartoon*, 70
carve *tiip*, 127
cash *okuk*, 118
cassava *iwa*, 95
cast *cast*, 70
castle *castle*, 70
cat *anwa*, 64
cataract *idwo mmong*, 88
catarrh *mkpoh*, 106
catch *kit*, 97
caterpillar *mkpo isang*, 104
cedi *cedi*, 70
cell *ufok mkpakop*, 132
centre *ufod*, 132
century *isua-ikie*, 93
cerium *cerium*, 70
chain *mkpọnọ*, 106
chair *nkpo itie ifum*, 89
chairman *obongowo obongowo*, 116
chairperson *obongowo obongowo*, 116
chairwoman *obongawan obongawan*, 116
chalk *eto nwed*, 81
champion *andikan*, 63
change *kpoho*, 99
change *ukpuhore*, 134
chaotic *timere*, 127
chapter *iwod-nwed*, 95
character *edu*, 77
characteristic *characteristic*, 71
charcoal *nkang*, 111
charge *odudu*, 116
chariot *chariot*, 71
chase *biine*, 69
cheap *bak*, 67
cheat *utuk*, 137
cheater *ama-iban*, 63
check *nwed-okuk*, 114
cheek *mfuk*, 103
cheese *cheese*, 71
chemistry *chemistry*, 71
chest *esit*, 80
chew *ta*, 126
Chewa *Chewa Chewa*, 71
chicken *unen unen*, 135
chief *obong*, 42, 116
chimpanzee *idiok*, 87
chin *mfuk*, 103
China *obio idung obio idung*, 115
chlorine *chlorine*, 71
chocolate *chocolate*, 71
choose *diangare*, 73
chorus *ikwo*, 90
Christmas *Emana-abasi*, 79
chromium *chromium*, 71

chronic *okposong*, 118
church *ufok abasi*, 132
cigarette *sika*, 123
cilantro *cilantro*, 71
circle *ikpu-ikpu*, 90
citizen *unie-obio*, 136
city *obio*, 115
civilized *ifiok*, 88
claim *nam*, 107
clap *mia*, 103
clarion *clarion*, 71
class *itie ukpep mkpo itie ukpep mkpo*, 94
classroom *ufok ukpep mkpo*, 133
clay *mbad*, 101
clean *kuhore*, 100
clean *sana*, 122
cleanliness *sana*, 122
clear *kponno*, 99
clear *ngwanga*, 110
clearly *awangha*, 65
click *fik*, 83
climb *faap*, 83
clinic *ufok ibok*, 132
clock *nkanika nkanika*, 111
close *bed*, 68
cloth *ọfọng*, 117
clothes *ofong ofong*, 117
cloud *ikpa enyong*, 90
cloud *ikpa enyoung*, 90
cloud computing *cloud-computing* 71
cloudy *tongo*, 128

coat *coat*, 71
cobalt *cobalt*, 71
cockroach *mfem*, 103
cocoa *cocoa*, 71
coconut *isip mbakara*, 93
cocoyam *ikpong*, 90
coffee *kọfi*, 97
coin *okuk*, 118
cold *ndedeng*, 107
collect *bo*, 69
collection *boi*, 69
college *ufok-nwed*, 133
colour *eyen-mkpo*, 82
colour *mme utor mme utor*, 106
comb *edisat*, 76
combine *dian*, 73
come *di*, 12, 15, 36, 54, 72
comfort *idongesit*, 88
comfort *ndongesit*, 109
comfortable *suugho*, 126
coming *di*, 72
command *uko*, 16, 134
commend *toro*, 128
commerce *udua*, 131
committee *mme adaha*, 106
communication *nneme*, 112
community *efak*, 77
company *itie utom*, 94
compensation *eno-ndongesit*, 80
competence *ukeme*, 133
çompetition *nduba*, 109
compound interest *compound-interest*, 71

comprehension *ofuri ofuri*, 117
computer *computer akeme iko*, 61
computing *computing*, 71
concern *ubehe ubehe*, 129
conclusion *akpatire*, 62
condolences *ekom*, 78
confidence *idorenyin*, 88
confusion *timede*, 127
congenial *congenial*, 71
Congo *obio idung*, 115
Congo-Brazzaville *Congo-Brazzaville*, 71
conjunction *conjunction*, 71
connection *mmum ndian mmum ndiàn*, 107
conscience *conscience*, 71
consequence *mkpo-ntipe*, 105
consist *si-isine*, 123
consonant *consonant*, 22, 71
constituency *constituency*, 71
construct *nam*, 107
contempt *ndisua*, 109
content *si-isine*, 123
continue *ka-iso*, 96
contract *contract*, 71
control *kara*, 96
conversation *nneme*, 112
converse *neme*, 110
cook *tem*, 126
cool *deghe*, 72
cool *fuuro*, 84
coop *coop*, 71

cooperation *cooperation*, 71
copper *copper*, 71
corner *mben*, 102
cornerstone *itiat ubedmkpo*, 94
corpse *akpo-owo*, 62
correct *nne-nne*, 112
corruption *ngwo*, 110
cost *kpa*, 98
Cote d'Ivoire *obio idung*, 115
couch *mkpo-itie*, 105
cough *ikong*, 89
count *bat*, 67
country *obio*, 115
courage *ukeme*, 133
courageous *uko*, 134
court *esop*, 81
cousin *ayen ayeneka ete ayen eyeneka ete(eka)*, 66
cover *fuuk*, 84
cover *ukọp*, 134
cow *enang*, 80
cowhide *ikpa enang*, 90
crab *isobo*, 93
crawl *nyoon*, 115
create *bod*, 69
creation *bod*, 69
creative *ubod mkpo*, 129
creativity *creativity*, 71
crime *idiok-mkpo*, 88
crocodile *effiom*, 77
cross *kpagha*, 98
crow *kpọk*, 99
crowd *umiang-owo*, 135

crown *anya anya anya-anya*, 64
cry *tua*, 128
cube *nkwa*, 112
cucumber *mfri mfri*, 103
culture *ido*, 88
cunning *nkara*, 111
cup *kọọp*, 98
cup *okop iko mmong*, 89
curiosity *itong*, 94
curium *curium*, 71
currency *okuk*, 118
curtain *ofong usung ofong usung*, 117
cushion *ekpat ofong*, 79
customer *adap-mkpo*, 58
cut *kpi*, 99

d *d*, 71
daily *usen*, 136
dam *dam*, 72
dance *unek*, 135
dangerous *adiọk*, 59
dark *kim*, 97
darkness *ekim*, 78
darmstadtium *darmstadtium*, 72
data *data*, 72
date *ma*, 101
date *usen-ọfiọng*, 136
daughter *ayin awowan*, 67
dawn *siere*, 39, 123
day *usen*, 38, 136
daybreak *usiere*, 136
dead *akpa*, 61
death *mkpa*, 104

debt *isung*, 93
decade *isua-duop*, 93
decay *biara*, 68
December *offiong duopeba*, 40, 116
decision *uyime*, 138
decrease *teghe*, 126
deduct *sio*, 124
deep *atongho*, 65
deer *ebet*, 75
defecate *toro*, 128
defile *biad*, 68
definition *mkpo-awongho*, 105
deflate *woro*, 140
degree *certificate*, 70
delightful *ndiyene-inem*, 109
delivery *ndinoh*, 108
demand *ndi-yem*, 108
democracy *democracy*, 72
deny *kang*, 96
dependable *dud ayen*, 74
deplete *uyaha*, 138
deposit *deposit*, 72
deposit *ndikpe okuk*, 108
depth *depth*, 72
descend *soyo*, 125
description *dokko yaha mkpo-aba*, 73
descriptive *dokko yaha-aba*, 73
desert *nsad-isọng*, 112
deserve *odot*, 116
design *design*, 72
desirable *udong*, 130

INDEX – INDEX

desire *wut*, 140
destiny *uwa*, 137
development *kpuho*, 99
device *device*, 72
devour *dia-sop*, 72
dew *mmong*, 106
diarrhoea *udongo utoro*, 131
dictionary *nwed ikó nwed iko*, 114
die *kpa*, 98
different *asong*, 19, 65
difficult *asong*, 65
difficulty *ọkpọsọng*, 118
dig *dok*, 73
dignify *ukpono*, 134
dignity *kpono*, 99
dimwit *useme*, 136
dine *udia mbebri-eyo*, 130
director *ada-usung*, 58
dirty *mbat*, 102
disabled *owo udongo*, 119
disappear *sop*, 124
disappoint *biat*, 69
discard *sio*, 124
disciple *mme mbet*, 106
discipline *kpan*, 98
discussion *ting*, 127
disease *udongo*, 131
disgrace *suene*, 125
disgusting *dienne*, 73
dishevelled *suagha*, 125
dishonor *una-ukpono*, 135
dishonour *usung-eyen*, 137
dispute *niin*, 111

distance *kpaat*, 98
distinguished *asanga*, 64
district *efak*, 77
diverse *kutor-kutor*, 100
diversity *ubanga*, 129
divide *siaak*, 123
divine *asangasanga*, 64
division *baanga*, 67
divorce *ndikpọng-ndọ*, 108
do *nam*, 107
doctor *nam nor*, 42, 107
document *document*, 73
dog *ebua*, 13, 35, 75
doll *nsek ayen akpo*, 112
dollar *dollar*, 74
donkey *enang mbiomo*, 80
door *udok usung*, 130
doubt *niin*, 111
doughnut *doughnut*, 74
dove *ibiom*, 86
down *isong*, 93
downward *downward*, 74
dowry *okuk-ndọ*, 118
doze *idap*, 87
drain *sio*, 124
drama *drama*, 74
draw *dut*, 75
dream *dapa*, 72
dress *ofonq ofonq*, 117
drink *ngwong*, 15, 36, 110
drive *wad*, 139
drop *tó*, 127
drown *mmong aben*, 106

drowsiness *idap*, 87
drum *ibit*, 86
drummer *amia-ibit*, 63
drunkard *ngwong kpa*, 111
dry *saat*, 122
dubnium *dubnium*, 74
duck *unen abeke*, 135
dump *imuum*, 91
dust *ntong*, 113
Dutch *Nederlands*, 109
duty *utom*, 137
DVD *DVD*, 75
dysprosium *dysprosium*, 75

each *keere-keet keere-keet*, 97
each and everyone *owo keere keed* 119
ear *utong*, 46, 137
early *bak*, 67
earring *mkpan utong mkpan utong* 104
earthenware *earthenware*, 75
east *east*, 40, 75
East Timor *east-timor*, 75
eastern *eastern*, 75
easy *mmeme*, 106
eat *dia*, 11, 15, 36, 54, 72
economy *economy*, 75
education *ufok-nwed*, 133
ee *i*, 85
efficiency *efficiency*, 77
effort *ukeme*, 133
egg *nsen unen*, 113
eight *itia-ita*, 37, 93

eighteen *efureta*, 37, 77
eighteenth *efid eta*, 77
eighty *anaang*, 38, 63
einsteinium *einsteinium*, 77
Ekua *Ekua*, 79
elastic *uduk akpó*, 131
elbow *ekong ubok*, 78
elder *ekamba owo*, 78
election *election*, 79
electric *ikang*, 89
electricity *idektrik*, 87
electron *electron*, 79
electronic *idektronic*, 87
element *element*, 79
elephant *enin*, 80
'eleven *duopekiet*, 37, 75
eleventh *duop-o-kiet*, 75
email *email*, 79
emancipator *emancipator*, 79
'embrace *fad*, 83
Emmanuel *Emmanuel*, 80
empathy *esit-mbom*, 80
emphasis *yiré*, 141
employee *ono-utom*, 118
employer *ono-utom*, 118
empty *ngkanga*, 110
end *akpatere*, 62
enemy *usua*, 136
energetic *odudu*, 116
energy *odudu*, 116
engine *ngine*, 110
engineer *ngineer*, 110
England *England*, 80

English *iko mbakara*, 89
enjoy *ndia uwem*, 108
enter *duk*, 74
entertaining *usio-mbire*, 136
entire *afed*, 59
environment *nto*, 113
envy *usin-eyen*, 136
equal *ukem*, 133
eraser *usok-mkpo*, 136
erbium *erbium*, 80
err *due*, 74
essential *akpan mkpo*, 61
eternal *nsinsi*, 113
eternity *nsinsi*, 113
Europe *europe*, 82
europium *europium*, 82
evening *ndubire*, 39, 109
event *edinam*, 76
everlasting *nsi-nsi*, 113
every *kpukpru*, 99
everyone *kpukpru owo*, 99
everywhere *afit-itie*, 60
evil *idiok*, 87
ewe *uman-edong*, 135
exam *udomo*, 130
example *uwud-mkpo uwud mkpo* 138
excellent *eti*, 81
exchange *kpugho*, 99
excuse me *sik-da*, 123
executioner *executioner*, 82
exit *woro*, 140
expense *ubiad-okuk*, 129

expensive *nsongurua*, 113
experience *ifiok*, 88
explain *temme*, 127
explanation *siaak*, 123
explode *sakka*, 122
extinguish *gwod*, 85
exult *dara*, 72
eye *eyen*, 82
eyeball *nkwa eyen*, 112
eyebrow *nwa eyen*, 114
eyelash *nwa eyen*, 114

f *f*, 82
fabric *ofong*, 117
face *iso*, 93
fade *kpa*, 98
fairness *afia*, 59
faith *mbuotidem*, 102
falcon *inuen*, 92
fall *duo*, 74
falsification *nsu*, 113
familiar *diongho*, 73
family *ufok emana ufok*, 132
family *ufok emana*, 41
famous *owuo iso- owo*, 119
, farm *iwang*, 95
farmer *otor iwang*, 42, 119
fart *mmiong*, 106
fast *suóp*, 126
fasting *utid-udia*, 137
fat *itene*, 93
father *ette ette*, 82
father *ette*, 41

father-in-law *ete ebe ette ebe(awan)* 81
fatigue *mba*, 101
favour *mfon*, 103
fear *baak*, 67
fear *ndik*, 108
February *Offiong Iba*, 39, 117
feedback *iboro*, 86
feel *kop*, 98
feeling *kop*, 98
fees *okuk*, 118
female *awowan*, 66
fermium *fermium*, 83
fertile *uforo*, 133
festival *usoro*, 136
fetish *mkpo-ibok*, 105
fever *ufiop idem*, 132
fifteen *efut*, 37, 77
fifteenth *efid*, 77
fifty *aba-ye-duop*, 38, 58
fight *ngwana*, 110
figure *ibad-mkpo*, 86
fill *sin*, 124
filthy *mbad*, 101
find *yum*, 141
fine *afon*, 60
finger *nnuon ubok*, 112
finish *ma*, 101
Finnish *Suomi*, 126
fire *ikang*, 89
first *akpa*, 61
firstborn *akpa-eyen*, 61
fish *iyak*, 41, 95

fisherman *ókó-iyak*, 42, 117
fishing-net *fishing-net*, 83
five *itin*, 36, 94
flag *flag*, 83
flat *kpaaba*, 98
flatulate *nyai*, 114
flee *feghe*, 83
flesh *obuk*, 116
flexible *amem*, 63
flicker *ngwene*, 110
flirting *akpara*, 62
flood *ndiọng*, 108
floor *isong*, 93
flow *woro*, 140
flower *uyai mfang*, 138
fluorine *fluorine*, 83
fly *furo*, 84
fog *ntukko*, 113
fold *fut*, 84
follow *keene*, 97
food *udia udia*, 130
food *udia*, 11, 16, 35, 54
fool *useme*, 136
foolish *siime*, 123
foot *ikpat*, 90
football *fịt-bọọt*, 83
for *ke*, 96
forbid *edikan*, 76
force *udit*, 130
foresee *kit*, 97
forest *akai*, 60
forever *nsi-nsi*, 113
forget *fire*, 83

INDEX – INDEX

forgive *daha*, 72
forgiveness *ndahare- nno*, 107
fork *asara-ikpang*, 64
forty *aba*, 38, 58
forward *nyan*, 114
foul *idiok ufik*, 87
found *kid*, 97
four *inang*, 36, 91
fourteen *duopenan*, 37, 75
fourteenth *duop enaang*, 74
fourth *inang*, 91
fowl *unen*, 135
fox *fox*, 84
fragrance *ufik*, 132
fragrant *ufik*, 132
framework *kpana*, 98
francium *francium*, 84
fray *fray*, 84
free *uboho*, 129
free *ufang*, 131
freedom *uboho*, 129
freezing *ndedeng*, 108
French *french*, 84
French *owo-french*, 119
friction *friction*, 84
Friday *ayoho usen ituon ke udua*, 39, 67
fried-fish *ufrafirai-iyak*, 133
friend *ufan ufan*, 131
friend *ufan*, 22
friendly *eti-ido*, 81
friendship *ufan*, 131
frighten *frighten*, 84

frightening *frightening*, 84
frog *ekwod*, 79
from *mmor*, 107
fruit *nfere*, 110
fruitful *fruitful*, 84
frustration *iyaresit*, 95
fry *frang*, 84
fuck *ukung*, 134
fufu *usung*, 137
Fula *fula*, 84
fulfill *akem*, 61
full *ayoho*, 67
fun *nem*, 110
funeral *usoro-mkpa*, 136
funny *inam*, 91
future *ini-iso*, 92

g *g*, 84
GaDangme *Gadangme*, 84
gadolinium *gadolinium*, 84
gain *uduk*, 131
gallium *gallium*, 84
gallon *okpo*, 118
game *mbere*, 102
Gandhi *Gandhi*, 84
gap *mkpafang*, 104
garage *ufok-motor*, 133
garden *iwang eben esa inwang*, 92
garden egg *nya*, 114
gari *gari*, 84
gaseous *gaseous*, 84
gather *kpuut*, 99
gaudy *nkeng-idem*, 111

Gbe *Evegbe*, 82
gecko *etuk-akpok*, 82
generation *emana*, 79
generosity *eti-uwem*, 81
Genesis *yenesis*, 141
gentle *sung*, 125
geography *geography*, 84
geometry *geometry*, 84
germanium *germanium*, 84
Germany *Germany*, 84
germinate *kord*, 98
get *yene*, 16, 140
Ghana *Ghana*, 84
giant *okposong*, 118
gift *eno*, 80
ginger *ginger*, 84
giraffe *giraffe*, 84
girl *nka-iferi awowan*, 66
girl *nka-iferi*, 12, 13, 35
girlfriend *ufan owowan ufan awonwan*, 131
give *noono*, 16, 42, 112
giver *andinọọ*, 63
global warming *global-warming*, 85
glorify *kom*, 97
glossy *yama*, 140
glutton *ekpe-udia*, 79
go *kaa*, 40, 96
goal *goal*, 85
goat *ebot*, 75
God *Abasi*, 58
godspeed *obong-osop*, 116

gold *gold*, 85
gold *uyai-mkpo*, 138
gong gong *gong-gong*, 85
good *eti mkpo*, 11, 13, 35, 55, 81
good *eti*, 81
good afternoon *etiero*, 81
good evening *good-evening*, 85
good job *eti-utom*, 81
good morning *emesiere*, 79
goodbye *ka di*, 48, 96
goodness *eti*, 81
gospel *iko-abasi*, 89
gossip *baanga*, 67
gossip *ndọk*, 109
govern *kara*, 96
governance *ukara*, 133
government *ada ukara*, 58
grab *mum*, 107
grace *mfon*, 103
gracious *mfon*, 103
graduate *ata ifiok*, 65
grain *mkpasip*, 104
grandchild *ayeyen*, 66
granddaughter *ayeyen ayeyen*, 66
grandmother *ekam*, 78
grandpa *etebom*, 81
grandson *ayeyen ayeyen*, 67
grape *urak-ayaebot*, 136
grasp *grasp*, 85
grass *mbiod*, 102
grasshopper *atak-tak*, 65
gratitude *ekom*, 78

grave *udi*, 130
grease *adan*, 58
great *okposong*, 118
greatgrandchild *udod ayeyen udod ayeyen*, 130
greed *itong*, 94
greedy *inọọk*, 92
green *awawa*, 41, 65
greet *kom*, 97
greeting *ekom*, 78
grey *iwat*, 95
grieve *seme*, 123
grind *kok*, 97
groin *groin*, 85
ground *isọng*, 93
groundnut *mmasang*, 106
group *atu*, 22, 65
grow *koot*, 98
growth *koot*, 98
guard *ukpeme*, 134
guava *wọfa*, 140
guess *keere*, 97
guide *kpeme*, 99
guilt *ndudue*, 109
Guinea-Bissau *Guinea-Bissau*, 85
guinea-fowl *unen abeke*, 135
guitar *guitar*, 85
gun *ikang*, 89

h *h*, 85
habit *edu owo*, 77
habitat *habitat*, 85
hafnium *hafnium*, 85
hair *ided*, 87

half *ubak*, 38, 129
hallelujah *hallelujah*, 85
hammer *hammer*, 85
hand *ubok*, 40, 129
handkerchief *ofong inua ofong inua*, 117
hang *koop*, 98
happen *tibe*, 127
happiness *inemesit*, 91
happy birthday *inemesit usen emana*, 91
happy new year *idaresit afa isua*, 87
harass *fana*, 83
harbour *esuk*, 81
hard *asong*, 65
hard *osong*, 118
hardship *nsọngọ-mkpọ*, 113
harmattan *ekarika*, 78
hassium *hassium*, 85
hassle *fana*, 83
hat *itam*, 93
hate *sua*, 125
hatred *sua*, 125
Hausa *Acusa*, 58
have *yene*, 38, 140
have a hold on *yene-a-mum-ke*, 141
having *tuagha*, 128
hawk *inuen*, 92
he *anye*, 14, 34, 54, 64
head *ibuot*, 46, 86
headache *ubiak ibuot*, 129

headphone *headphone*, 85
headscarf *mbop-ibuot*, 102
heal *kuk*, 100
healing *osong*, 118
health *idem*, 87
heap *kup*, 100
hear *kop*, 98
heart *esit*, 80
heartbreaker *abung owo-esit*, 58
heat *ufiop*, 132
heaven *edem-eyong*, 76
heavy *udob*, 130
hedgehog *hedgehog*, 85
heel *etetighe*, 81
height *idagha*, 87
helicopter *ubom onyong*, 129
helium *helium*, 85
hello *aloo*, 48, 63
help *unwam*, 136
help *wam unwam*, 136
hemisphere *ufọt-eyọng*, 133
hen *unen*, 135
her *anye*, 64
her *enye*, 14, 34, 80
herb *nkong ibok*, 111
here *mi*, 16, 36, 103
here *mmi*, 106
hero *akoñko*, 61
herring *nyoo*, 115
herself *eye*, 82
hi *hi*, 85
hide *dibe*, 73
high-school *secondary school*, 123

highlife *highlife*, 85
highway *usung*, 137
him *anye*, 64
himself *eye*, 82
hiplife *hiplife*, 85
hippopotamus *isantim*, 92
his *enye*, 14, 34, 80
history *mbok*, 102
hit *kpokko*, 99
hold *mum*, 107
hole *ndudu*, 109
holiday *nduk-odudu*, 109
holmium *holmium*, 85
holy *edisana*, 76
home *ufok ufok*, 132
home *ufok*, 12, 54
honesty *eti-uwem*, 81
honey *adan-akuok*, 58
honour *kpono*, 99
hope *idorenyin*, 88
horn *horn*, 85
horse *enang*, 80
hospital *ufok ibok*, 132
hot *ufiop*, 132
hotel *itie udia uwem*, 94
hour *ini*, 38, 91
house *ufok ufok*, 132
house *ufok*, 13, 35, 54
housekeeper *akpeme ufok akpeme ufok*, 62
how *die*, 73
how are you *idem mfó*, 87
how much *uwak*, 138

INDEX – INDEX

hug *fad*, 83
huge *akamba*, 60
human *owo*, 119
humankind *awo*, 66
humble *suugho*, 126
humiliation *suene*, 125
humility *nsuhuridem*, 113
hundred *ekpad-nniara*, 38, 78
hunger *abiong*, 58
hungry *biong*, 69
hunter *ata utop ata utop*, 65
hurry *sop*, 124
husband *ebe ebe*, 75
hut *atayat*, 65
hydrogen *hydrogen*, 85
hypocrisy *nkara*, 111

I *i*, 11, 14, 34, 48, 54, 85
I am well *idem mmi osong*, 87
ice *ice*, 86
ice-cream *icecream*, 86
idea *ifiok*, 88
ideal *ideal*, 87
idiom *idiom*, 88
if ... then *edien*, 76
if *akpe-do*, 62
Igbo *Uneghe*, 135
iguana *iguana*, 89
illness *udongho*, 130
immerse *immerse*, 90
immigrant *immigration*, 91
impact *akpan mkpo*, 61
imperfection *imperfection*, 91
important *akpan mkpo*, 62

in *ke*, 96
inactive *abiara*, 58
incinerate *ndifop-mkpo*, 108
inclusion *sin*, 124
income *uduk*, 131
increase *tot*, 128
independence *dod-eyen*, 73
India *India*, 91
Indian *Indian*, 91
Indian *indian*, 91
indigent *uwene*, 138
indigo *indigo*, 91
indium *indium*, 91
infect *nnor*, 112
infertile *ikemke ndibon*, 89
infinity *nsi-nsi*, 113
information *stop*, 16, 125
infrastructure *infrastructure*, 91
ingratitude *idiok-esit*, 88
inheritance *inyene ufok*, 92
inject *kim*, 97
injection *ibok*, 86
injure *unan*, 135
inlaw *ukot*, 134
insect *insect*, 92
insinuate *wana ndi ting*, 139
insult *miom*, 103, 104
insults *usong-eyen*, 136
integrate *dian*, 72
intelligent *ifok*, 88
interest *udod*, 130
international *otu mme obio*, 119
internet *internet*, 92

INDEX – INDEX   164

introduction *editongo*, 77
invest *invest*, 92
investment *inyene*, 92
invoice *invoice*, 92
iodine *iodine*, 92
Iphone *iPhone*, 92
iridium *iridium*, 92
iron *ukwak*, 134
Islam *Islam*, 93
Islamic *Islamic*, 93
island *island*, 93
issue *mfana*, 103
it *ite*, 93
it *mkpo*, 42, 55, 104
italiano *Italiano*, 93
its *anye*, 64
its *mkpọ*, 104
Itsekiri *Itsekiri*, 94
itself *itself*, 95
ivory *ivory*, 95

j *j*, 95
jaguar *jaguar*, 95
jama *jama*, 95
January *Offiong Kiet*, 39, 117
Japan *japan*, 95
Japanese *Japanese*, 95
jar *atu*, 65
jealousy *idiok esit*, 87
Jerusalem *Jerusalem*, 95
Jesus *Eyin-obong*, 58
jewelry *jewelry*, 95
job *utom*, 137
Johannesburg *johannesburg*, 95

John *Yohn*, 141
join *dian*, 22, 73
joke *nyọọ*, 115
journey *usung isang usung isang*, 137
joy *inemesit*, 91
judge *kpe*, 98
July *Offiong Itiaba*, 40, 117
jump *tama*, 126
junction *junction*, 95
June *offiong itiokeed*, 40, 117
just *ado*, 59
just *just*, 95
justice *ikpe*, 90

k *k*, 96
keep *kama*, 96
Kenya *Kenya*, 97
kerosene *mmong ikang*, 107
key *ukpohore*, 134
khakhi *afong*, 60
kid *eyin ekpri eyen*, 79
kid *eyin*, 41
kidnapping *ndiyiip-owo*, 109
kill *wot*, 140
kind *aduuk*, 59
kind *etido*, 81
kindergarten *kindergarten*, 97
kindle *kindle*, 97
kindness *etido*, 81
king *edidem*, 76
kingdom *obio*, 115
kiss *tom*, 128
kiss *tum*, 128

kitchen *ebiet unam udia ufok utem mkpo*, 75
knee *edong*, 46, 77
knife *ikua*, 90
know *fiok*, 83
knowledge *ifiok*, 88
Kofi *Kofi*, 97
kola nut *efiat*, 77
Kongo *kongo*, 98
Konkomba *Likpakpaln*, 100
koran *koran*, 98
Krio *krio*, 99
krypton *krypton*, 99
Kweku *Kweku*, 100

l *l*, 100
lab *lab*, 100
laboratory *itie-usio-iyip*, 94
ladle *ikpang*, 90
lady *aboikpa*, 58
lake *mmong itie kiet*, 107
lamb *nyen-edong*, 115
land *isong*, 93
landlord *unie-ufok*, 136
language *iko*, 22, 89
lanthanum *lanthanum*, 100
large *akamba*, 60
last *akpatire*, 62
lastborn *asanga-edem*, 64
later *yak amana*, 140
laugh *saak*, 122
laughter *imam*, 90
law *mbed*, 102
lawrencium *lawrencium*, 100

lawyer *akpe-ikpe*, 62
lay *bit*, 69
laziness *ifu*, 88
lazy *ifu*, 88
lead *ngket*, 110
leader *ada-ibout*, 58
leadership *ada ukara*, 58
leaf *mfang*, 103
lean on *bere*, 68
learn *kpem*, 54, 99
learning *ukpep*, 134
leather *leather*, 100
leave *kpong*, 99
ledge *ledge*, 100
left *ufiin*, 40, 132
leg *ukot*, 134
lemon *lemon*, 100
lend *wuot*, 140
length *length*, 100
lens *umono-eyen*, 135
leopard *leopard*, 100
leprosy *akpa-mfia*, 61
Lesotho *lesotho*, 100
lesson *ukpep mkpo*, 134
let ... know *neme*, 110
let *yak*, 140
letter *nwed-etop*, 114
lettuce *ikong*, 89
levy *okuk mbet*, 118
liability *uko*, 134
liar *osu-nsuk*, 119
liberty *unen*, 135
library *itie-ukodnwed*, 94

lick *ngweem*, 110
lid *ukup*, 134
lie *sugho*, 125
life *uwem*, 138
lifetime *ini uwem*, 91
lift *kpappa*, 98
light *uwana*, 138
lightning *akeb keb*, 61
lightweight *nyahade mkpo*, 114
like *ma*, 101
lily *lily*, 100
lime *mkpri sokoro*, 106
line *line*, 101
Lingala *Lingala*, 101
link *link*, 101
lion *ekpe*, 79
lip *mkpok inua*, 106
lipbalm *udot-inua*, 131
liquid *mmong*, 106
liquor *mmin*, 106
listen *kop*, 98
lithium *lithium lithium*, 101
litigate *faanga*, 82
little *ekpri*, 79
little *ndiyiip-owo*, 109
live *due*, 74
liver *liver*, 101
living *du*, 74
living-room *living-room*, 101
lizard *ekpok*, 79
loan *ewuoot*, 82
lobster *isobo*, 93
location *itie*, 94

lockdown *lockdown*, 101
locust *ngkukumkpoyoriyo*, 110
log in *log-in*, 101
log out *woro*, 140
logo *logo*, 101
loin *edak*, 76
Lomwe *Lomwe*, 101
London *Obio-mfia Obio-Mfia*, 116
long *nyoong*, 115
look *se*, 122
loosen *tad*, 126
Lord *Obong*, 116
lose *duook*, 74
lot *uwak*, 137
loud *mkpo*, 104
louse *ndang*, 107
love *ima*, 11, 15, 35, 54, 90
lover *ma*, 101
loyal *usuku ibuot*, 137
lung *lung*, 101
lutetium *lutetium*, 101

m *m*, 101
machine *ngine*, 110
madam *eka ufok*, 77
made up *nam-eyong*, 107
magazine *nwed-mbok*, 114
magnesium *magnesium*, 101
maid *eyen-ufok*, 82
mail *mail*, 101
main *ata amor*, 65
maintain *nim*, 111
maize *ebikpod*, 75
major *akpan mkpo*, 61

make *nam*, 107
make love *nam-ima*, 107
maker *andibod*, 63
malaria *uto-eyen*, 137
male *awoden*, 66
male *eden owo*, 76
man *awoden*, 66
manage *tuko*, 128
management *andikara*, 63
manager *ada iwud*, 58
manganese *manganese*, 101
mango *manko*, 101
manner *edu-unam mkpo*, 77
many *uwak*, 138
map *map*, 101
March *Offiong Ita*, 117
march *offiong ita*, 117
marijuana *marijuana*, 101
Mark *idiongho*, 88
mark *idiongho*, 88
market *udua*, 131
marriage *ndo*, 109
marry *ndo*, 109
mask *mkpo ufuk iso mkpo ufuk iso*, 105
massive *ekamba*, 78
masticate *ta-mkpo*, 126
mate *nka*, 111
material *mkpo utom*, 105
maths *ibad*, 86
Matthew *Matthew*, 101
mattress *mbid*, 102
maximum *ekamba*, 78

May *akeme inam*, 40, 61
maybe *akeme ido*, 61
me *ami*, 63
mean *oworo*, 119
meaning *oworodidie*, 119
measure *domo*, 74
meat *unam*, 41, 135
medicine *ibok*, 86
meet *kid*, 97
meitnerium *meitnerium*, 103
melayu *melayu*, 103
melon *ikon*, 89
melt *yet*, 141
member *owo*, 119
memorization *tiyo*, 127
memorize *keere*, 97
memory *iwuot*, 95
mendelevium *mendelevium*, 103
mental *mkpo nsup*, 105
mention *siaak*, 123
mercury *mercury*, 103
mercy *mbom*, 102
mere *nkanga*, 111
merry *daara*, 72
message *etop*, 81
messenger *isang-utom*, 92
metal *ukwak*, 134
metre *metre*, 103
microphone *mkpo-uting-iko*, 105
middle *ufuot*, 133
milk *mmóng eba*, 107
millet *millet*, 103
million *million*, 103

mind *esit*, 80
mine *eke mi*, 78
minimum *ekpri*, 79
mint *mint*, 103
minute *ini*, 91
mirror *ukut iso ukid iso*, 133
miser *uma*, 135
miserly *uma*, 135
miss *due*, 74
miss *wond*, 140
mistake *ndudwe*, 109
mister *uma*, 135
mix *waak*, 139
modern *afa eyo*, 11, 59
Modern Greek *ellinika*, 79
Mohammed *Mohammed*, 107
molecule *molecule*, 107
molybdenum *molybdenum*, 107
mom *eka*, 77
moment *idagha*, 87
Monday *akpa usen ke udua akpa usen ke udua*, 61
Monday *akpa usen ke udua*, 39
money *okuk*, 118
monkey *ebok*, 75
month *okuk udongo*, 118
moon *offiong*, 116
more *awak*, 65
more *uwak*, 138
morning *ubaha-usen*, 39, 129
mosque *itie-ukpono*, 94
mosquito *ọbọng*, 116
motorcycle *mkpo isang*, 104

mountain *obod*, 116
mouse *ekpoh*, 79
mouth *inua*, 46, 92
mouthful *ekpri-mkpọ*, 79
move *sang*, 122
movie *ndise*, 108
mud *mbat*, 102
multiplication *dian*, 72
mum *ama*, 41, 63
murder *ndi ewod owo*, 108
mushroom *udip*, 130
music *ikwo*, 90
muslim *muslim*, 107
mustache *idet-inua*, 87
mute *imuum*, 91
my *mmi*, 14, 34, 106
myself *mmi*, 106
mystery *ndidibe-mkpo*, 108

n *n*, 107
nail *mbara*, 102
nail *ukwak*, 134
name *eyin aying*, 67
name *eyin*, 49
Namibia *Namibia*, 107
nation *obio*, 115
national *national*, 107
nausea *udong-ekikoi*, 130
navel *ekop*, 78
Ndebele *Ilimi*, 90
neck *itong*, 94
necklace *mkpo itong*, 104
need *udong*, 130
needle *uween*, 138

INDEX – INDEX

negative *negative*, 109
neighbour *ndung-ndiana*, 109
neighbourhood *mbók-idung*, 102
neodymium *neodymium*, 110
neon *neon*, 110
nephew *ayen awoden ayeneka ete,eka* 66
neptunium *neptunium*, 110
network *network*, 110
neutron *neutron*, 110
never *ikemeke*, 89
nevertheless *ndien*, 108
new *ufa*, 14, 35, 131
news *etop*, 82
newspaper *nwed-etop*, 114
next *efen*, 77
nice *eti*, 81
nickel *nickel*, 111
niece *ayen awowan ayeneka ete,eka* 66
Nigeria *Obio-Nyin*, 116
Nigerian *obio*, 115
night *okoneyo*, 39, 118
nine *usukkiet*, 37, 137
nineteen *efurenan*, 37, 77
ninety *anan-ye duop*, 38, 63
niobium *niobium*, 111
nitrogen *nitrogen*, 111
no *iyo*, 16, 36, 49, 95
Noah *Noah*, 112
nobelium *nobelium*, 112
noise *uyom*, 139
nominate *sio*, 124

nonsense *ndisiime*, 108
normal *ntoro*, 113
north *north*, 40, 112
northern *northern*, 112
Norway *Norway*, 112
nose *ibuo*, 46, 86
not *idoho*, 88
notebook *nwed*, 114
nothing *mkpo-idoho*, 105
noun *noun*, 112
November *offiong duopkiet*, 40, 117
novice *afa-owo*, 59
number *ibad-mkpo*, 86
numbness *ibikpai*, 86
nurse *ukuk udongoh*, 42, 134
nursery *nursery*, 114
nut *isip*, 93

ỏa *o*, 115
oath *ewongho*, 82
obedience *nkop-item*, 111
obey *kpono*, 99
objective *aim*, 60
objective *objective*, 116
obviously *awaha*, 65
ocean *akpa*, 61
October *offiong duop*, 40, 116
odd *odd*, 116
of *ake ake*, 60
office *ufok utom*, 133
often *tiaara*, 127
Oganesson *oganesson*, 117
oil *adan*, 58

okay *okay*, 117
okro *etike*, 81
old *akaan*, 14, 35, 60
old lady *akan-awan*, 60
old man *akan-eden*, 60
on *ke*, 15, 96
one *keed*, 96
one *kiet*, 13, 35, 37, 97
one person *owo-kiet*, 119
onion *oyim*, 119
open *kuppo*, 100
oppose *oppose*, 118
opposite *nsaha-iso*, 112
or *mmi doho*, 106
orange *sokoro*, 124
order *uyio*, 138
order *uyo*, 139
organ *organ*, 118
organization *itie utom*, 94
organizer *organizer*, 118
Osita *Osita*, 118
osmium *osmium*, 118
ostentatious *nsio*, 113
other *efen*, 77
our *nnyin nnyin*, 112
our *nnyin*, 14, 34
ourselves *nyin*, 115
outside *esion*, 80
overflow *aneke-yoho*, 63
overgrow *aneke-akpon*, 63
oware *nsa-isong*, 112
owe *kama*, 96
owl *nkid-ikid*, 111

owner *unie*, 135
ox *enang*, 80
oxygen *oxygen*, 119

p *p*, 119
pacify *book*, 69
page *ikpa nwed ikpa nwed*, 90
pail *akpo-mmong*, 62
pain *ubiak*, 129
painful *biak*, 68
paint *kpen*, 99
paint *paint*, 119
palace *ufok-obong*, 133
palladium *palladium*, 119
palm *eka esit ubok*, 77
palmnut soup *efere-abak*, 77
palmwine *ukot-nsung*, 134
pan *esuo-uframkpo*, 81
Panjabi *punjabi*, 121
paper *ikpa nwed*, 90
parable *ngke*, 110
parched *parched*, 119
parent *ete ye eka ette ye eka*, 81
parent *ette ye eka*, 82
parents *unie-eyen*, 135
park *park*, 119
parliament *ufok-mbed*, 133
parliamentarian *parliamentarian*, 119
parrot *inim*, 92
part *itie*, 94
partner *partner*, 119
party *party*, 119
pass *biyo*, 69

pass by *biyo*, 69
passion *udong*, 130
passport *ndise*, 108
paste *dian*, 72
pastor *etubom*, 82
path *mkpafang*, 104
patience *ime*, 90
patient *owo-udongho*, 119
pauper *uweene*, 138
pawpaw *bobo*, 69
pay *kpe*, 98
payment *ndikpe-okuk*, 108
peace *emem*, 79
peck *tum*, 128
pedophile *pedophile*, 120
peel *kuoi*, 100
peer *nka*, 111
pen *eto nwed*, 81
pencil *eto uwed nwed*, 81
penguin *penguin*, 120
penis *mfet*, 103
people *mme owo*, 106
pepper *ntukon*, 114
peppermint *peppermint*, 120
perfume *perfume*, 120
period *ini*, 91
permanent *nsinsi*, 113
permission *odudu*, 116
persecute *yire*, 141
person *owo*, 11, 35, 55, 119
personal protective equipment *ppe*, 120
pet *ufene*, 132

Peter *peter*, 120
petition *petition*, 120
philanderer *akpara*, 62
philosopher *philosopher*, 120
phone *mkpo utang-iko*, 105
phosphorus *phosphorus*, 120
photograph *ndise*, 108
physics *physics*, 120
piano *piano*, 120
pick *been*, 68
picture *ndise ndise*, 108
Pidgin English *pijin*, 120
pig *edi*, 76
pigeon *tomtom*, 128
piggy bank *piggy-bank*, 120
pillar *abai*, 58
pillow *udori ibuot mkpo udod ibut*, 105
pinch *yiip*, 141
pineapple *pinable*, 120
pink *pink*, 120
pins and needles *unuen-ye-unuen*, 136
pioneer *akpa-owo*, 61
pipe *akpor*, 62
pipe *smoking-pipe*, 124
pitiful *mbom*, 102
pito *pito*, 120
place *ntie ntie efe*, 113
place *ntie*, 15, 16
plan *kere*, 97
plane *ubom-eyong*, 130
planet *ererimbot*, 80

plant *toh*, 41, 127
plantain *ukom*, 134
plate *usan udia usan*, 136
platinum *platinum*, 120
play *bire*, 69
play *mbire*, 102
pleasant *nneenem*, 112
please *mbok*, 48, 102
pledge *pledge*, 120
plentiful *uwak*, 138
pluck *kekpe*, 97
plutonium *plutonium*, 120
pocket money *pocket-money*, 120
poem *poem*, 46, 120
point *nyan*, 114
poke *saap*, 122
police *udo-obod*, 130
policy *ido*, 88
political party *politicalparty*, 120
politician *politician*, 120
pollution *idiok-afum*, 87
polonium *polonium*, 120
poop *ifuo*, 89
poor *weene*, 139
population *ibad-owo*, 86
porcupine *porcupine*, 120
pork *unam*, 135
porridge *mbot*, 102
position *idagha*, 15, 87
possess *mkpo-nsop*, 105
possessive *possessive*, 120
pot *esio*, 80
potassium *potassium*, 120

potty *asana*, 64
pound *tim*, 127
pour *duoi*, 74
poverty *uweene*, 138
powder-keg *powder-keg*, 120
power *odudu*, 116
powerful *odudu*, 116
praise *ekom*, 78
praseodymium *praseodymium*, 120
prawn *prawn*, 120
pray *akam*, 60
prayer *akam*, 60
preach *kuoro*, 100
predict *dioho*, 73
pregnancy *idip*, 88
pregnant *yommo*, 141
prejudice *prejudice*, 121
preparation *beenge*, 68
preparations *beenge*, 68
prepare *beenge*, 68
preserve *nim*, 111
president *ada ukara*, 58
press *fik*, 83
press *press*, 121
pretend *nkara*, 111
pretty *uyai*, 138
prevent *kpeme*, 99
previous *akan*, 60
price *udua-mkpo*, 131
pride *mkpon*, 106
priest *aku*, 42, 62
primary school *ufok nwed ntok*

eyen, 132
prince *ayin-ọbọng*, 67
print *print*, 121
printer *printer*, 121
prison *mkpokobo*, 106
problem *mfana*, 103
proceed *ka-iso*, 96
process *nam*, 107
producer *producer*, 121
product *mkpo udua*, 105
profit *uduk*, 131
programme *edinam*, 76
progress *uforo*, 133
project *edinam*, 76
promethium *promethium*, 121
promise *ewongó*, 82
promise *kaanga*, 96
pronoun *pronoun*, 121
prop *prop*, 121
property *iyene*, 95
prophesy *nkikid*, 111
prophet *akid-nkikid*, 61
prosperity *iyene*, 95
protactinium *protactinium*, 121
protect *bem*, 68
protection *ukpeme*, 134
proton *proton*, 121
proverb *nké*, 111
provide *nor*, 112
prudence *inyene-ifiọk*, 92
pull *dud*, 43, 74
punish *tuko*, 128
puppet *puppet*, 121

purchase *deb*, 72
purple *purple*, 121
purpose *ntak*, 113
pursue *yire*, 141
push *nua*, 43, 114
put *sin*, 124
puzzle *puzzle*, 121

q *q*, 121
quake *earthquake*, 75
quality *eti mkpo eti mkpo*, 81
quantity *ukpa*, 134
question *mbeme mbeme*, 102
question *mbeme*, 16
quick *soop*, 124
quickly *sop*, 124
quiet *dob*, 73
quotation *quotation*, 121

r *r*, 121
rabbit *eku mbakara*, 79
race *itók*, 94
radiation *radiation*, 121
radio *ekebe uting iko akeme uting iko*, 61
radium *radium*, 121
radon *radon*, 121
rain *edim*, 76
rainbow *rainbow*, 121
rainy *edim*, 76
rainy season *ukwo-edim*, 135
raise *dakada*, 72
raisin *raisin*, 121
rand *rand*, 121

rap *suop*, 126
rape *ina nkan-ubok*, 91
rape *ina-nkanubok*, 91
rat *ekpu*, 79
raw *ndek*, 108
razor *razor*, 121
reach *sim*, 123
reach a final milestone *sim-à-akpatere-ntor*, 123
read *kud*, 42, 45, 55, 100
reading *kod*, 97
real *ataa*, 65
reality *ataa*, 65
rear *anan*, 63
rearguard *ukpeme-ekọng*, 134
reason *ntak*, 113
rebel *rebel*, 121
rebellion *rebellion*, 121
receive *bó*, 69
record *record*, 121
recover *yene*, 141
rectangle *rectangle*, 121
red *idaidat*, 41, 87
reduce *sio*, 124
refrigerator *ekebe ntuhube*, 78
registration *ugwed-anying*, 133
regret *mkpefiok*, 104
reign *ba*, 67
reject *nyeme*, 115
rejoice *daara*, 71
relationship *ndubeghe*, 109
relative *eyin-eka*, 82
reliable *reliable*, 121

remain *bed*, 68
remember *tee*, 126
remind *toyo*, 128
remote control *remote-control*, 121
remove *sio*, 124
repair *diong*, 73
repeat *fiak-nam*, 83
repent *kappa-esit*, 96
replace *sin*, 124
reply *iboro*, 86
report *doho*, 73
report *iboro*, 86
representative *uwud-mkpo*, 138
reputation *ekikere ke baha owo*, 78
request *bip*, 69
requester *andibip*, 63
rescue *yaha*, 140
resemble *biet*, 69
resent *iyaresit*, 95
resentment *iyaresit*, 95
respect *kpono*, 99
respond *boro*, 70
response *iboro*, 86
responsibility *ubók utom*, 129
responsible *ubiong utom*, 129
rest *duk-udod*, 74
restaurant *itie-udiamkpo*, 94
result *resuts*, 86
resurrection *sed*, 123
retail *sio-nyam*, 124
return *return*, 121

INDEX – INDEX

reveal *nwud*, 114
revive *deme*, 72
rhenium *rhenium*, 121
rhodium *rhodium*, 122
rice *edesi*, 76
rich *imọ*, 91
riddle *nke*, 111
right *nen*, 110
right *udom*, 40, 130
rights *nen*, 110
ring *mkpa-inuun*, 104
ringworm *ekpo mfem*, 79
ripen *daat*, 72
rise *kokko*, 97
risk *risk*, 122
river *inyang*, 92
road *usung*, 137
roam *yong*, 141
roast *fop*, 83
rock *itat*, 93
rocket *rocket*, 122
roentgenium *roentgenium*, 122
Romans *Romans*, 122
roof *eyong okom eyong okom*, 82
room *ubed ubed*, 129
roost *ufok inuen*, 132
root *aduñ*, 59
rope *uduk*, 131
rot *buto*, 70
row *ndisi*, 108
rubbish *ndisime*, 108
rubidium *rubidium*, 122
ruin *biad*, 68

rule *ukara*, 133
run *feghe*, 83
ruski *Ruski*, 122
ruthenium *ruthenium*, 122
rutherfordium *rutherfordium*, 122

s *s*, 122
sabotage *biad*, 68
sack *sio ke utom*, 124
sacrifice *wa*, 139
sad *fugho*, 84
safe *sung*, 125
safety *sung*, 125
salary *okuk-offiong*, 118
salt *inung*, 92
salutation *ekom*, 78
salvation *eriyaha*, 80
samarium *samarium*, 122
same *ukem*, 133
sand *ntan*, 113
sanitizer *sanitizer*, 122
sarcasm *sarcasm*, 122
Saturday *ayoho usen itiokiet ke udua*, 39, 67
sauce *sauce*, 122
saucepan *ban*, 67
save *nyianga*, 115
saving *ubók-akuk*, 129
saviour *andiwam*, 63
say *yumo*, 141
say goodbye *wara*, 139
scandium *scandium*, 122
scar *mbon*, 102
scarce *mbon*, 102

scarcity *una*, 135
scare *ndo*, 109
scarlet *idaidat*, 87
scary *ndik*, 108
scatter *suaan*, 125
school *ufok-nwed*, 35, 123
science *science*, 122
scissors *ufad-mkpo*, 131
scoop *koi*, 97
scooter *mkpọ-isang*, 105
score *sin*, 124
scorn *ndisong-eyen*, 108
scorpion *mbamba*, 102
scrape *kuat*, 99
scream *bong*, 69
scrub *sok*, 124
sea *akpa*, 61
seaborgium *seaborgium*, 122
search *yum*, 141
seat *ifum*, 89
second *eba*, 75
second *iba*, 85
secret *ndedibe*, 108
security *akpeme-itie*, 62
see ... off *suk*, 125
see *se*, 122
seed *mkpasi*, 104
seek *yum*, 141
seizure *udongho*, 130
seldomly *nsubó*, 113
select *sat*, 122
selenium *selenium*, 123
selfishness *uyim*, 138

sell *nyam*, 114
seller *ayam-udua*, 66
send *dong*, 74
sense *kop*, 98
sentence *iko*, 89
September *offiong usukkiet offiong usukkiet*, 117
September *offiong usukkiet*, 40
sequence *sequence*, 123
serious *song-odudu*, 124
serve *efak*, 77
service *edere*, 76
set *nehe*, 109
settle *kwehe*, 100
seven *itia-aba*, 37, 93
seventeen *efid-eba*, 37, 77
seventy *ata-ye-duop*, 38, 65
several *umiang*, 135
sew *kim*, 97
sex *ina*, 91
sex education *sex-education*, 123
sh *sh*, 123
shade *eyen-mkpo*, 82
shake *nyek*, 114
shame *buut*, 70
share *deeme*, 72
sharpen *ban*, 67
she *anye*, 14, 34, 54, 64
sheabutter *sheabutter*, 123
sheep *edong*, 77
shield *mkpọ-ukpeme*, 105
shine *yama*, 140
ship *ubom nsungikang*, 129

shirt *itong ofong*, 94
shit *afit*, 60
shoe *ikpaukot ikpa ukot*, 90
Shona *Shona*, 123
shoot *top*, 128
shop *ufok urua ufok udua*, 133
shopping *udebep*, 130
short *ibio*, 86
shorts *ofong ukot*, 117
shoulder *afara*, 46, 59
shout *mkpo*, 104
show ... pity *mbom*, 102
show *wut*, 15, 140
shower *ufok uyere idem ufok uyere idem*, 133
shower *yeh*, 140
shrimp *abu*, 58
shrink *fiim*, 83
shut *kuuk*, 100
shut down *kuuk*, 100
shyness *beud beud*, 68
sibling *ndito eka*, 109
sick *udongo*, 131
sickness *udongo*, 131
sigh *sioop*, 124
sign *sign*, 123
signify *idiongho*, 88
silent *dobo*, 73
silicon *silicon*, 123
silver *silver*, 123
simple *idaha-idaha*, 87
sin *dwe*, 75
sing *kwo*, 100

sing jama *kwo-jama*, 100
singing *kwo*, 100
sink *deeng*, 72
sink *mkpo nyed usan*, 105
sister *eyeneka-awowan ayeneka awowan*, 66
sit *tie*, 15, 36, 127
six *itiokeed*, 36, 94
sixteen *efutkiet*, 37, 77
sixteenth *efutkiet*, 77
sixty *ata*, 38, 65
skeleton *okpo*, 118
skill *uso*, 136
skin *ikpa idem*, 90
skirt *ofong idem*, 117
sky *ikpa enyoung*, 90
slap *ufia*, 132
sleep *idap*, 87
sleep tight *nna-fon*, 112
slice *kpeke*, 99
slim *nsip- nsip*, 113
slippers *ikpa ukot*, 90
slow *sung-sung*, 126
slowly *sung-sung*, 125
slut *akpara*, 62
small *ekpri*, 79
smart *diongho- mkpo*, 73
smash *nuakka*, 114
smell *ufik*, 132
smile *tebe*, 126
smoke *nsungikang*, 113
smoothen *dono*, 74
snail *ekwong*, 79

snake *uduk-ikot*, 131
sneeze *waya*, 139
snore *nkon*, 111
snow *ekarika*, 78
snowy *ekarika*, 78
soaked *udebe*, 130
soap *suob suop*, 126
social distancing *nsan nsan*, 112
sock *fip fip*, 83
sodium *sodium*, 124
sofa *mkpo itie*, 104
soft *mem*, 103
soften *mmeme*, 106
soil *ererimbot*, 80
soldier *owo-ekong*, 119
solemn *akpan mkpo*, 62
solution *iboró*, 86
some *ubaak*, 129
someone *owo*, 119
something *mkpo*, 104
sometimes *ubak-ini*, 129
somewhere *somewhere*, 124
son *ayin awoden*, 67
song *ikwo*, 90
soothe *sukho idem*, 125
soothing *sung*, 125
sorrow *seme*, 123
sorry *kpe*, 48, 98
Sotho *Sotho*, 125
soul *ukpong*, 134
sound *uyom*, 139
soup *efere*, 77
source *source*, 125

south *south*, 40, 125
South Sudan *South-Sudan*, 125
southern *southern*, 125
sow *toh*, 127
space *afang*, 59
space *ufang*, 131
spade *udók*, 130
spank *ufia*, 132
spatula *ekpang*, 78
speak *tang*, 19, 126
spear *eduat*, 77
special *asaha-saha*, 64
speed *suóp*, 126
spend *biad*, 68
spending *biad*, 68
spider *ndukóm-ekpe*, 109
spine *akpo asak-edem*, 62
spinning top *spinning top*, 125
spirit *ukpong*, 134
split *siaak*, 123
spoil *biara*, 68
sponge *nkpo uyet usan kusà*, 100
sponsor *andiwam*, 63
spoon *ikpang ikpang*, 90
sport *sport*, 125
spouse *ebe ebe(awan)*, 75
spread *swan*, 126
spring *spring*, 125
sprout *tibe*, 127
sputum *ikong*, 89
spy *se*, 122
squeeze *nyimme*, 115
squirrel *adua*, 59

stab *kim*, 97
stadium *Akwa anwa mbre*, 63
stamp *dian*, 72
stand *da*, 71
star *nta nta offiong*, 113
start *tuho*, 16, 128
state *obio*, 115
statement *iko*, 16, 89
station *ntor ndaha*, 113
stay *dong*, 74
steal *yib*, 141
steer *steer*, 125
step *step*, 125
step-child *ayen ebe ayen ebe (awan)* 66
stepfather *ebe awan ebe awan*, 75
stew *efere*, 77
stick *eto*, 81
still *asoho*, 65
stimulate *udong*, 130
stinginess *uyim*, 138
stink *tebe*, 126
stir *kama*, 96
stomach *idip*, 88
stomach-ache *ubiak-idib*, 129
stone *itiat*, 93
stool *ifuọ*, 89
stop *biere*, 69
store *udua ufok udua ufok*, 131
storehouse *udua ufok*, 131
storm *oduma*, 116
story *uto*, 137

stove *nkpo utem udia*, 112
straight *anyan*, 64
straighten *nen*, 110
strange *esen*, 80
stranger *asen*, 64
street *usong*, 136
strength *odudu*, 116
strengthen *udud*, 131
stress *ufen*, 132
stripe *stripe*, 125
striped *dud*, 74
strive *nwana*, 114
stroll *isang*, 92
stroll *sanga*, 122
strong *song*, 124
strontium *strontium*, 125
structure *shape*, 123
student *eyen-ufoknwed*, 82
studio *itie-utom*, 94
study *kpeep*, 98, 99
stumble *duo*, 74
subtract *sio*, 124
success *uforo*, 133
such as this *utor-nte-ayem*, 137
suck *fiip*, 83
suckle *fiip*, 83
sue *kop*, 98
suffer *ufen*, 132
suffering *ufen*, 131
sugar *suka*, 125
sugarcane *mboko*, 102
sulfur *sulfur*, 125
sum *ibad okuk*, 86

summarisation *summarization*, 125
summer *nda-eyo*, 107
sun *offiong*, 116
Sunday *edere*, 39, 76
sunny *utin*, 137
sunrise *nda eyo*, 107
support *nwam*, 114
surpass *kan*, 96
surround *yuhu*, 141
sushi *sushi*, 126
swallow *meenge*, 103
swallow *men*, 103
Swati *Swati*, 126
swear *wogho*, 140
sweep *kuok*, 100
sweet *inem*, 91
sweet potato *inem-udia*, 91
sweetheart *inighe*, 92
swim *wok*, 140
switch off *nime*, 111
switch on *domo*, 74
symbol *idiongho*, 88
syringe *unnuen*, 136

t *t*, 126
table *okpokoro okpokoro*, 118
tablet *nkwa-ibok*, 112
tail *isim*, 93
take *been*, 43, 68
Takoradi *Takoradi*, 126
talk *ting*, 127
tall *nyoong*, 115
tantalum *tantalum*, 126

tap *inua mmong*, 92
taste *kop*, 98
tattered *taagha*, 126
tax *okuk mbet*, 118
taxi *mkpo isang*, 104
tea *ti*, 127
teach *kpem*, 99
teacher *akpep-nwed*, 42, 48, 62
team *otu*, 119
tear *waak*, 139
tease *dong*, 74
technetium *technetium*, 126
technique *usung-edinam*, 137
technology *dioho-die*, 73
technology *technology*, 126
teenage *ufa-aboikpa*, 131
telephone *mkpo uting iko*, 105
telescope *telescope*, 126
television *ekebe ndise akeme ndise*, 61
tell *doho*, 73
tellurium *tellurium*, 126
temple *obot-abasi*, 116
ten *duop*, 37, 74
tent *ufok mkpo*, 132
terbium *terbium*, 127
test *domo*, 74
test *udomo*, 130
thallium *thallium*, 127
than *akan*, 60
thank *kom*, 97
thank you *afo*, 46, 48, 60
thanks *sosongoh*, 124

thanks *sosongo*, 124
that *anye*, 64
that *aye*, 49, 66
that escalated quickly *eye-adok-usop*, 82
the *ko*, 11, 13, 54, 97
theatre *itie-usiak-idem*, 94
theft *ino*, 92
their *mmo*, 14, 35, 106
them *mmo*, 106
themselves *idem-mmor*, 87
then *ndien*, 108
therapist *okuk-udongho*, 118
there *do*, 16, 36, 73
therefore *therefore*, 127
these *eyem*, 82
they *nmo*, 14, 34, 54, 112
thicken *tok*, 128
thief *ino*, 92
thin *asip*, 65
thing *mkpo*, 104
think *keere*, 97
thinking *keere*, 97
thirst *udong*, 130
thirteen *duop ita*, 37, 74
thirteenth *duop ita*, 74
thirtieth *edip-mme-duop*, 76
thirty *edip-ye-duop*, 37, 76
this *enyem*, 45, 80
this *eyem*, 82
thorium *thorium*, 127
thought *akikere*, 61
thousand *ikie*, 38, 89

thousands *tosin*, 128
threat *threat*, 127
three *ita*, 36, 93
thrive *foro*, 84
throat *itong*, 94
throne *ifum-ukara*, 89
throw *top*, 128
throw away *top-duook*, 128
thulium *thulium*, 127
thumb *nnuon ubok*, 112
thunder *aduma*, 59
thunderbolt *thunderbolt*, 127
Thursday *usen inang ke udua*, 39, 136
tidy *asana*, 64
tie *bop*, 69
time *ini*, 15, 38, 91
times *ini*, 91
timetable *ini-mkpo*, 92
tin *iko*, 89
tiny *epire*, 80
tire *kak*, 96
tiredness *kak*, 96
titanium *titanium*, 127
tithe *tithe*, 127
to *ke*, 96
tobacco *ike*, 89
today *mfin*, 103
toe *ukot*, 46, 134
toffee *toffee*, 127
together *diana-kiet*, 73
toilet *ufok uka ifuo*, 133
toilet roll *mkpo ukuhore efod mkpo*

ukuhore efod, 105
tolerance *yo*, 141
tomato *tomato*, 128
tomorrow *mkpong*, 11, 15, 36, 55, 106
tongue *edeme*, 76
too *nde*, 107
too much *uwak*, 138
tool *mkpo-utom*, 105
tooth *eded*, 76
toothbrush *nkpo utuk edet mkpo usok inua*, 105
toothpaste *mkpo usok inua*, 105
topic *ibio-iko*, 86
torment *tuko*, 128
total *afed*, 59
touch *tuuk*, 129
tough *osong*, 118
tour *tour*, 128
towel *ofong ukwohore idem ofong ukohore idem*, 117
town *obio*, 115
trade *ndiyam*, 109
trade *ndubeghe*, 109
trader *ayem udua*, 42, 66
trading *ndubeghe*, 109
tradition *mbed*, 102
traffic *traffic*, 128
train *mkpo isang*, 104
train *train*, 41, 128
transform *kpuho*, 99
translate *kapa*, 96
translation *kapa*, 96
translator *akapa-iko*, 60
transportation *transportation*, 128
trash *mkpo-mbio*, 105
travel *daka*, 72
travel *dakka*, 72
treason *biangha*, 68
treasure *ma*, 101
treat *nam*, 107
tree *eto eto*, 81
tree *eto*, 13, 35
tremble *nyek*, 114
triangle *anen ita*, 63
tribute *iko-ekom*, 89
trick *nkara*, 111
trillion *trillion*, 128
triumph *kan*, 96
trouble *mfana*, 103
trouser *ofong ukot ofong ukot*, 117
truck *truck*, 128
true *akpaniko*, 62
trumpet *aduk*, 59
trust *mbutidem*, 103
trust *nem*, 109
truth *akpaniko*, 62
try *nwana*, 114
tuberculosis *akpaikpai-ikong*, 61
Tuesday *ayoho usen iba ke udua*, 39, 67
Tumbuka *tumbuka*, 128
tungsten *tungsten*, 128
turbulent *mfana*, 103
turkey *turkey*, 129
turn off *nime*, 111

turtle *ekwod-mmong*, 79
tweet *tweet*, 129
twelfth *twelfth*, 129
twelve *duopeba*, 37, 75
twenty *edip*, 37, 38, 76
twin *amana iba*, 63
twist *fiak*, 83
two *iba*, 36, 37, 85
type *utor*, 137

u *u*, 129
ukelele *ukelele*, 133
umbilicus *ekop*, 78
umbrella *ufuk-eyo*, 133
uncle *ayeneka ete,eka awoden*, 42, 66
under *idaak*, 86, 87
understand *anwanga*, 64
underwear *ofong idak idem*, 117
undesirable *undesirable*, 135
unemployed *una utom*, 135
unfamiliar *ndiohoke*, 108
ungrateful *ungrateful*, 135
union *diana-kiet*, 73
unite *diana*, 73
unity *diana*, 73
universe *unadot*, 135
unkempt *asere*, 64
unnecessary *ibaha-ufọn*, 86
ununtrium *ununtrium*, 136
up *eyong*, 82
upright *nne-nne*, 112
uranium *uranium*, 136
urinate *tok*, 128

urine *ikim*, 89
us *afed*, 59
USA *USA*, 136
usage *kama*, 96
use *kama*, 96
user *andikama*, 63

v *v*, 139
vaccinate *unor ibok*, 136
vaccine *editibe*, 76
vagina *itit*, 94
valiant *valiant*, 139
value *mma*, 106
value *utum-kama*, 137
van *mkpo isang*, 104
vanadium *vanadium*, 139
vase *iko flower*, 89
vehicle *mkpo isang*, 104
vein *asip*, 65
Venda *venda*, 139
venom *venom*, 139
ventilator *mkpo-usin ebifik*, 105
venue *itie*, 94
verandah *esa*, 80
verb *verb*, 15, 139
verse *ufang*, 131
very *tutu*, 129
very much *umiang*, 135
vibrate *nyek*, 115
victory *kan*, 96
video *video*, 139
village *idung*, 88
vim *vim*, 139
violence *afai*, 59

violet *violet*, 139
virtue *eti*, 81
virus *udongo udongo*, 131
vision *nkikid*, 111
visit *ke-se*, 96
vitality *song*, 124
voice *uyo*, 139
vomit *kok*, 97
vote *fik-ubọk*, 83
vote *ufik-ubok*, 132
voucher *nwed-akuk*, 114
vowel *vowel*, 22, 139
vulture *utede*, 137

w *w*, 139
waah *waah*, 139
waist *isin*, 93
wait *bet*, 68
wake *toi*, 127
wake up *deme*, 72
walk *isang*, 92
wall *ndibene*, 108
walnut *ekom*, 78
want *yum*, 12, 36, 141
war *ekong*, 78
warehouse *ufok ubon-mkpo*, 132
warn *kpan*, 98
warning *kpan*, 98
warrior *owo ekong*, 119
wash *yet*, 141
wasp *ataat*, 65
wasted *uyagha*, 138
watch *bem*, 68
water *mmong*, 41, 106

watermelon *watermelon*, 139
wave *fim*, 83
way *usung*, 137
we *nnyin*, 14, 19, 34, 54, 112
weak *mem*, 103
wealth *imo*, 91
weapon *mkpo ekong*, 104
wear *sine*, 124
weather *ayio*, 67
weave *dok*, 73
web *web*, 139
website *website*, 139
wed *do*, 73
wedding *ndó*, 109
Wednesday *ayoho usen ita ke udua*, 39, 67
wee hours *ubiak-usen*, 129
weed *mbiet*, 102
week *udua*, 131
weigh *domo*, 74
weight *udop*, 131
welcome *emedi*, 48, 79
well *afon*, 60
well *ọfọn*, 117
west *west*, 40, 139
wet *ndedeng*, 107
what *nsido*, 16, 49, 113
when *idaha ke*, 87
when *ini-ke*, 92
where *nmor*, 112
which *eyeke*, 82
whine *nyiik*, 115
whip *ikpa*, 90

white *afia*, 13, 35, 54, 59
who *anie owo*, 63
whole *afed*, 59
whose *anie*, 63
why *ntaha*, 113
wicked *ibaak*, 85
wide *ufang*, 131
widow *ebe kpa*, 75
widowed *ebe-kpa*, 75
widower *awan akpa*, 65
wield *wield*, 139
wife *awan*, 65
wild *idiok*, 87
will *will*, 139
win *kan*, 96
wind *afim*, 59
window *usung afum*, 137
windy *afem*, 59
wine *mmin*, 106
wing *mbai*, 101
winter *ekarika*, 78
wipe *kuohode*, 100
wisdom *ifiok*, 88
wise *ifiok*, 88
wish *duak*, 74
wish *udong*, 130
witch *ifot*, 88
witchcraft *ifot*, 88
with *ye*, 140
withdraw *sio*, 124
witness *ntiensé*, 113
wolaytta *wolaytta*, 140
woman *owo uwan ekamba awowan*, 78
womb *itie-eyen*, 94
wonderful *mkpa idem*, 104
wood *eto*, 81
word *iko iko*, 89
work *utom utom*, 137
work *utom*, 137
worker *anam-utom*, 63
workshop *itie-ubokutom*, 94
world *ererimbot*, 80
worm *utung*, 137
worry *fana*, 83
worship *kpono*, 99
wow *iya*, 95
wring *furo*, 84
wrist *itong ubok*, 94
write *wet*, 19, 42, 139
writer *awed nwed*, 42, 66
writing *nwed*, 114
wrong *dwe*, 75
wrongly *dwe*, 75

x *x*, 140
xenon *xenon*, 140
xylophone *ikon*, 89
xylopia *xylopia*, 140

y *y*, 140
Yaa *i*, 85
yam *bia*, 68
yard *yaat*, 140
yawn *adunwan*, 59
yaws *yaws*, 140
ye *ye*, 140

year *isua*, 39, 93
yell *bong*, 69
yellow *jellow*, 41, 95
yes *ntoro*, 16, 36, 49, 113
yesterday *mkpong*, 106
you *afo*, 14, 34, 54, 60
you *youes*, 141
you *youe*, 141
you *yous*, 14, 34, 54, 141
young *abaak*, 58
your *afo*, 14, 34, 49, 60
your *ake-mfo*, 14, 35, 61
yours *ake-mfo*, 61
yourself *idem-mfo*, 87
yourselves *idem-mfo*, 87
ytterbium *ytterbium*, 141
yttrium *yttrium*, 141

z *z*, 141
Zambia *Zambia*, 141
Zambian *zambian*, 141
zebra *zebra*, 141
zero *ikpu-ikpu*, 36, 90
Zimbabwe *Zimbabwe*, 141
Zimbabwean *Zimbabwean*, 142
zinc *zinc*, 142
zirconium *zirconium*, 142
zoology *zoology*, 142
Zulu *zulu*, 142

INDEX – INDEX

Iko Mbakara kasahorow

efi.kasahorow.org/app/l

- Efik Family Dictionary : Efik-English
- My First Efik Dictionary : Colour and Learn Efik

KWID: G-KKK25-EFI-EN-2022-08-01
www.kasahorow.org/booktalk
Afo! Thank you!

Printed in Great Britain
by Amazon